Our Administrative Pastor retired
... but God brought you, Pastor Jay
and Family. ...but God really cares.

Jim Sigel

But God . . .

Jim Seigel

authorHOUSE®

AuthorHouse™
1663 Liberty Drive
Bloomington, IN 47403
www.authorhouse.com
Phone: 1 (800) 839-8640

Published by AuthorHouse   09/15/2016

ISBN: 978-1-5246-3862-7 (sc)
ISBN: 978-1-5246-3861-0 (e)

Print information available on the last page.

This book is printed on acid-free paper.

Preface

In 2013, I began to feel that I was supposed to write an autobiography. I had no idea why, but when I mentioned this to my children and grandchildren, they unanimously agreed that I should. They must want to know what goes on in the mind of a retired CPA. I've never had a talent for writing, so the idea seemed a little unusual, but with the encouragement of my family, I went ahead and did it. I've never kept a diary, so only those things I can still remember are included. As such, when writing this book, I prayed that God would allow me to remember those things that were most important. I was indeed fortunate to have my granddaughter, Katie, who majored in English and Writing, to edit my book.

Me with Katie and Ann

Contents

1

A Beginning

● ● ● ● ● ● ● ● ● ● ●

I WAS BORN DECEMBER 14, 1935 at 119 E. Madison Street in Auburn, Indiana. My parents, Herman and Myrtle, named me James but called me Jimmy. I'm sure that they wished me to be a girl, since I was the fourth and last child and they already had 3 boys: Herman (Herm), Jr., born on August 28, 1928; Richard, born on March 3, 1930; and Robert (Bob), born on January 25, 1932. Several pictures at home showed me to be a blondie with long curly hair.

My dad was a hardworking man who had a job as a molder at the Auburn Foundry. I know he would have loved to have a job that wasn't so hard on his lungs, but Mom didn't want him to leave a steady job and risk unemployment, especially during the Depression. My mom took in laundry to wash, dry, and iron for people. She was a hard worker and had a number of steady customers. I remember that after we got television in the 50s, she would sit in front of the television set many nights ironing with a rotary iron. She would place clothes, sheets, or pillowcases in the roller and run them through a rather large press. She picked up the clothes from her customers, washed them, dried them (on the line either in the basement or outdoors), and then delivered them back to the customer. I'm sure that, even combined, both my parents' incomes were insufficient for a family of six.

My folks weren't rich in money, but they were rich in love. My brothers and I love our childhood memories, and we never lacked anything important. Mom and Dad were longtime members of Trinity Lutheran

Church in Auburn, an affiliate of the Lutheran Church, Missouri Synod. They were also staunch Democrats. I was baptized as a baby at Trinity, and was confirmed in 1948 after taking Confirmation classes.

I don't recall many of my experiences as a child. A few stand out, however. When I was about three or four, my parents became concerned about my vision. They had noticed visual defects and took me to an eye doctor, who suggested that I go to the Bluffton clinic. The doctor there suggested that I had a condition called Lazy Eye Syndrome. He gave my parents a black patch and told them to make me wear it over my left eye, saying that would make me use the right eye. Mom and Dad obliged, only to have me continually throw the patch in the coal bin. After I did this several times, they were puzzled. It took them some time to determine that I threw the patch away because I couldn't see. I even remember them saying, "Jimmy's a good boy. There must be some reason he's doing this." In a further checkup, it was finally determined that I was truly blind in my right eye.

Another memory that I recall occurred when I was six or seven and wanted to fool my dad. We had placed a grocery box in the living room, and I decided to hide in it while my dad was taking a shower in the basement. I apparently didn't do a very good job, because Dad knew exactly where I was. He pretended not to know and yelled at Mom that the box shouldn't be in the middle of the living room. He proceeded to pick up the box and said he was taking it to the burn pile. That scared me, so I jumped, causing him to lose control of the box and drop it. When I fell, I broke my arm and had to wear a sling for some time.

When I was about seven or eight years old, Bob was quarantined with scarlet fever. Richard and Herm were shipped out to the families of their friends, while Bob and I were unable to leave the house for several weeks, since Mom figured at my age, I should be at home. My memory of this is rather faded, but it seems to me that I was quite bored.

One day when I was about twelve years old, I was frustrated with my dad. I looked him in the eye and proclaimed, "Forty-five years old, and not a brain in your head!" It wasn't one of my better moments. I received a good whipping for that comment, and learned to respect my parents as a result.

Since I was the youngest of four boys, my three brothers were constantly teasing me and trying to stir up my temper. They regularly put horseradish in my mashed potatoes because they knew it would make me mad. One time I exploded and threw a spoonful at them. I missed and the potatoes splattered all over the wall. I don't know why I still remember that, but my outburst must have had some harsh consequences.

Another thing my brothers would do was wake me up when they got home from a date. They would tell me that it was time for school, when it was actually only about midnight. Since they were dressed, I would believe them, and once I finished dressing and getting ready, they would say they were just teasing and that I should go back to bed. I would always get so mad, which only encouraged them to play more pranks on me in the future.

Once I reached the age of ten or eleven, it was time for me to get a job. As my three brothers had done, I began caddying at the golf course, which was only a short walking distance north of where we lived. Some of the bags I carried were almost as large as I was. I remember early in my caddying career, I was caddying for two ladies and walking across the bridge on the 6th hole. I fell into the creek – bags and all. The sweet ladies told me to go home to get dry, and I think they even paid me for the full round, which was about 75 cents at the time. Caddies were picked on quite a bit; at least I was. I remember the other caddies making me crawl through their legs while they smacked me on my rear end. One time they even forced me to drink urine. Despite all of this, however, I still enjoyed caddying.

Following in my brothers' footsteps, I later did other jobs on the golf course. One year, I worked as salesman and clerk at the caddy shop, selling refreshments and golf supplies. For several years I worked on the greens committee, mowing the greens and cutting the rough areas. I remember on one occasion, I was cutting grass in the rough areas by hand and came across a snake. I have always been dreadfully scared of snakes. In this instance, I was so scared I ran out and waved down Chuck Blevins, a childhood friend, to trade me jobs. He was mowing fairways with a driving mower, which seemed much preferable to being anywhere near the snake.

In the summer of 1952, I worked from midnight to 8 a.m. six days a week, watering the greens and tees. At midnight I would put the sprinklers on the greens (nine holes one night and the other nine the alternate night). I would move them to other spots on the green at 1:30, 3:00, and 4:30, and then move them to the tees at 6:00. At 7:30, I rolled the hoses back up. I really enjoyed that job and very seldom fell asleep during the night. I think I took an alarm clock with me, because between shifts I would sit in the pro shop. I knew the golf course extremely well, so usually I would go from one green to the next without benefit of a light, although I carried one with me just in case. It also helped me see the various green positions for the sprinklers.

One night in particular stands out in my memory, though. That night it was so foggy I couldn't see my hand in front of my face. The flashlight did absolutely no good. I remember attempting to walk from 10 tee to 10 green, which would have been straight east, and walking into a sand trap nearly straight south. Fortunately, it was the only sand trap on the course with an island in the middle, so I knew I was at the side of the 15th green. From that, I knew that the clubhouse was directly north, possibly 150 yards away, and by feeling my way along a line separating fairway and rough, I was able to make it back to the pro shop. I don't remember how I finished the night, but I think the fog must have cleared at some point.

I didn't just work at the golf course, though. Another job I had as a boy was setting pins at the bowling alley. Jack Sanders, who was also pro at the golf course, was the owner of the bowling alley, which was above the Kroger Store on the southeast corner of 7th and Jackson Streets before moving to Sprott Street on Auburn's south side. Setting pins involved sitting in a booth beside the pin deck. The other boys and I would jump down, roll the ball back, and put the pins in the spots where they belonged. My friend, Chuck, was also setting pins in the alley adjacent to mine, and we used to race to see who could get the ball rolled back and the pins in their places first. Once, I was hurrying so fast that when I put the ball on the ramp to roll it back and leaned down to pick up the pins, the ball rolled back into the spot where I was kneeling. I am extremely competitive, and in my rush to win, I had not placed the ball firmly on the rack. It came down on my head and could have killed me if it had landed only a fraction of an inch over. *But God* prevented that from happening. Even so, I was unconscious and had to be carried out of the pit.

I hardly ever took time to be a kid. I was expected to work from a young age. My parents were poor, but I don't think I ever realized it. I don't regret working so much, however. It kept me out of trouble. I think these experiences gave me an advantage over other children, because I grew up knowing the value of money as well as the importance of having a good work ethic.

2

School Years

⬤　⬤　⬤　⬤　⬤　⬤

I GRADUATED FROM AUBURN HIGH School in May of 1953. My graduating class was made up of sixty-five students. Our class is still very active, and more than sixty-two years after leaving Auburn High, about fifteen of us get together four times each year. Children were much better controlled in the 40s and 50s since the teachers had more control than is allowed these days. Back then, we never heard of anyone using drugs, even in the major cities. A major offense in those days would be something like putting chewing gum on the bottom of a school seat or passing notes to another student. If ever a student were found pregnant, they usually went to live with someone out of town because of their humiliation. Things certainly were different back then.

From first through fourth grades, I attended Riley School (on the corner of 1st and Van Buren). I spent fifth and sixth grade at Desoto School (114 S Baxter Street), seventh and eighth grade at Auburn Junior High School (beside Harrison Elementary School), and ninth through twelfth grade at McIntosh High School. All four of these schools have since been torn down. I completed all twelve grades in twelve years, but was never a really good student, as my brothers Bob and Richard were. I now attribute that to being too young. I started first grade at the age of five, without attending kindergarten first. If I had been held back one year, I might have been a much better student, since I was a straight A student in college.

I don't remember much from grade school or high school, but I have a couple of memories. One is my very first day of first grade. When the bell rang for recess, I thought school was out for the day, so I went home. My mom was really upset about that and walked me back to school.

When I reached sixth grade, I was in a class with a couple of the boys who were always getting into trouble. Our teacher, who also happened to be the principal of DeSoto School, was an old man, probably seventy-five years old, and it was his job to answer the phone when it rang. The phone was outside the classroom in the main hall. Whenever he left the room to answer the phone, one of the two troublemakers in our class would take a yardstick and move the clock ahead ten minutes. Sometimes our class was actually over before the first grade class. I'll never know if our teacher was fooled or if he just went along with it in order to shorten our class time.

One of the other memories I have from school was the great basketball team Auburn had in 1949-1950. I was a freshman that year, and our "Red Devils" went to the state finals. This was quite an accomplishment for a school as small as ours; we only had about 125 boys in our entire high school. Indiana has always been known for the skill of its basketball teams, and I firmly believe that it is because most states had "class" basketball, which is where the tournaments are divided based on the size of each school. Indiana's tournaments had all schools playing against each other, regardless of size. This left our school of approximately 125 students competing against schools of all sizes. Although the chances of a small school winning a state title were rather small, it was a big deal when it did happen. This was quite an achievement for Auburn. Milan, a school in southwestern Indiana, achieved the same thing in 1962. Their entire high school had 162 enrolled, and they won the state tournament against the Muncie Bearcats, who had 1662 enrolled students. The movie *Hoosiers* was based on this event, and, in my opinion, is one of the best sports movies ever. In 1997, Indiana's tournaments changed to competition among schools of the same size, and the popularity of Indiana basketball has never been the same.

Although I was never good at competing in sports, I was certainly enthusiastic. One year, I was even a cheerleader. It wasn't for my jumping and acrobatics skills, but rather for my loud voice and enthusiasm. One sport I did participate in, however, was track, because all three of my brothers were good at running the mile. Richard and Herm were in the mile races at the same time for several years, and would always finish in first and second place. Crowds were larger when they ran just because many people went to see Herm and Rich race against each other. As I recall, one of them would win about half of the time, and the other the other half. I figured that if all three of my brothers were good at the mile run, I would also excel at it. The coach, aware that I was not as athletically gifted as I hoped, decided to let me go ahead and make a fool of myself. One time I was in a race against Bob. I think I was a sophomore and Bob was a senior. Near the end of the race, I looked ahead to see a beautiful sight: the finish line was just ahead, and no one was in front of me. Then I realized that I was on Lap 3 and Bob was on Lap 4. I didn't have the heart to break the string, so I stepped out of the way. I'm pretty certain that made the sports page and also ended my running career. From that point on, I focused on my own interests and decided to leave the running to my brothers.

3

College

GRADUATING HIGH SCHOOL, WHILE AN important milestone, turned out to be just the first step in becoming an adult. I had no idea what I was going to do after high school, but I decided that I should probably get a college education. In 1953 there were no guidance counselors, so since math was always my best and easiest subject, I asked the high school math instructor to give me advice on what to do in life. She considered my math skills and suggested engineering. My brothers Bob and Rich were at Purdue University, Rich in the field of engineering and Bob pursuing a teaching degree. So I applied to Purdue at West Lafayette, Indiana, as an Engineer candidate. I absolutely hated my first semester at Purdue. It was my first occasion being away from home, and I was homesick from the very first day. I questioned whether engineering was something I could enjoy or be successful in, especially when I discovered I was failing chemistry and drawing. I could not even envision how to draw the back of a block without turning the block around. *But God* had other plans for me. Knowing I would never make it as an engineer (I would surely have starved to death even if I could have graduated), I found out that I could take an aptitude test offered at Purdue. When my son, Jeff, later took an aptitude test, he found that he was equally good at almost any type of work, which I sort of envy. Not so with me. My aptitude for accounting was quite high. My aptitude for anything else was quite low.

As a result, I quit Purdue and immediately applied at Fort Wayne International Business College. It was a very small college located on the second floor of a building on the northwest corner of Washington and Harrison in Fort Wayne, Indiana. The college was offering only 1½ and 2-year degrees, but was considered by many to be a top college for accounting. The school offered only business administration, secretarial, business law, writing, cost accounting, industrial accounting, government accounting, and public accounting, but with all of the hours devoted to law and accounting, it probably offered as much accounting training as a 4-year college could.

After my second semester, a new semester began on June 5 of 1954. I was standing in the main assembly room when the newly arriving first semester students entered the hall. As I watched all of the new girls come in, I immediately noticed a beautiful blonde girl. I loved blondes. I was never a flirt or very bold, but I really wanted to meet this girl. So I said to myself, "Jim, sell her your books. You're finished with several of yours, and she's going to want to save money by buying used books." I wasn't aware at the time that her dad had suggested that she buy used books if she could. As it turns out, selling her my books was of the best decisions I have ever made. Not only was I able to introduce myself to her, but I was later able to spend time with her helping her understand her math and accounting lessons. What a beautiful Lord we serve.

4

Romance

● ● ● ● ● ● ● ● ● ● ●

ANN CERTAINLY APPEALED TO ME, but it was some time before we had a date because I had been dating a girl named Mary Lou from Zanesville. During the summer of 1954, there was to be a students' day with a golf activity in the afternoon and a prom that same evening. Somehow I was invited to join four of my accounting teachers for a round of golf in the afternoon, and I had invited Mary Lou to go to the prom with me that evening. I asked Ann if she would like to join me on the golf course, with me playing and her as a most beautiful companion. She agreed, to my delight. When we finished golfing, she asked me if I would take her to her cousin's home in Fort Wayne so she could get ready for the prom. What I didn't realize yet was that she assumed she was going with me to the dance. But as I was waiting in the car while she changed, it dawned on me that I was facing a serious dilemma. I had to tell her I would drop her off at the prom, but that I already had a date. Fortunately, even after I broke the news to her, Ann didn't give up on me (surely another *But God* moment). It was, however, the main topic of conversation for many of the students for some time. I've never been able to understand why almost everyone who hears this story thinks that I committed such a terrible sin. I don't remember asking Ann to go to the prom; I had simply asked her to walk around the golf course with me.

A short time later, Mary Lou told me that she had a boyfriend, Stanley, who had completed his time in the Navy and was returning home, so she and I wouldn't be dating any more. I apparently wasn't too upset, because the next day I shared the news with Ann, who was delighted. I told her I would like to come to her house on the following Sunday if it was okay with her. She was elated. Ann and I became much closer after this and had a few dates, although at this time I still was unaware that she was Catholic. I began to realize that I rather liked this girl. The only thing that bothered me was that I had seen her smoke several times, and I thought seeing a girl with a cigarette in her mouth was disgusting. I liked her enough to share my thoughts on the subject and found that she did not really care to smoke; she had just begun trying it out and was pleased to quit. Who knows whether she would have continued if I hadn't said something?

One of our first dates was with another student, Bill Bennett, and his girlfriend, Mona Lou. I remember that date especially well because when Bill made a left turn on DeWald Street from Calhoun Street, I gave Ann her first kiss, right on the lips! This may seem to have been a little quick, but although it was our first date, we had met and talked at school for quite a while.

After Ann and I started dating, I would go to her house almost every weekend, and, naturally, had met both of her parents. I saw her dad only a couple of times, though, before receiving a telegram one evening in September of 1954 saying that Ann could not keep our date because her father (whom everyone called Dutch) had died of a heart attack. I knew immediately that I should go and pay my respects. I don't think Ann expected me to show up at the funeral home, since it was so early in our relationship and I hardly knew her parents, but she was thrilled that I had come. She told me later that it was very important and meaningful to her.

I made lots of trips to her home on Third Street in Decatur. Sometimes I had to drink cold coffee and open the car windows to keep me awake on the way home to Auburn. At times I even listened to loud evangelistic sermons, not because I was interested in their content, but because they would help keep me alert (which says a lot about my religious state at the time). The weather also proved to be a challenge; sometimes the snow was so deep that I had to look at the telephone poles to find out where the highway was. I'm sure that this really worried both of our mothers, but I really wanted to get to Decatur.

My parents didn't want me to continue dating Ann since she was a Catholic. Lutherans were trained in those days to have no association with

Catholics, and for a Lutheran to date a Catholic was really a terrible thing in the eyes of Missouri Synod Lutherans. I had learned that too, but there was no way I was going to give up dating this beautiful blonde. Ann's mom also cautioned her against dating me. Once, Ann wrote me a letter asking me not to see her anymore because she felt our religious differences would create a problem. It was a hard decision for her to mail that letter, and she tells me she hated the fact that she did it, but she could hardly go to the post office and retrieve it. I was crushed, *but God* gave me insight to go to Decatur to see if I could change her mind. I found out that she had gone ice-skating to take her mind off of the letter, and I was able to locate the lake that she was skating on. Thank God that when she saw me she came skating over, rejoicing that I had come. Hallelujah!

Ann and I became quite serious, but faced a big problem because my parents were unwilling to give permission for us to marry. It wasn't that they didn't like Ann, just that they were worried about our differing religious beliefs. Despite this, they treated Ann well. As a matter of fact, they even took her with us on a vacation trip one time, and they would take her to Catholic services on Sunday mornings and pick her up when they were over. One Christmas she joined us for our family Christmas gift exchange, and my parents gave me a kitten. They had it in a package, and as I was preparing to open the package, the box moved, Ann screamed, and the kitten jumped out of the box and ran into the basement. It stayed in the basement hiding for several days before we could coax it back upstairs. Even though they included Ann in holidays and vacations, though, my parents continued to think it was a bad idea for me to marry a Catholic.

Actually, we were hearing more and more about marriage problems between Lutherans and Catholics. It became quite obvious that neither of us had a very good commitment to God, because we began discussing how we could make such a marriage work. I figured that mixed marriages failed because the Lutherans and Catholics continually argued over differences. Neither of us was willing to leave our church and attend the other's, but we reasoned that if we did not discuss God or religion, the differences would not be a problem. We agreed that neither of us would invite the other to attend our respective churches. After all, we figured, church was only an hour a week, two including Sunday school. We would each go to our own church and not discuss God for the remaining 166 hours of the week. I would not change from Lutheran to Catholic, but signed a paper agreeing to raise our kids Catholic. At that time, the Catholic Church would not marry a couple unless the non-Catholic agreed to sign such a document. At least it settled the matter so we wouldn't argue about it when the time came.

After dating Ann for about sixteen months, I knew that I wanted Ann to be my wife. We had both discussed the issue a number of times, but I decided to propose on a night that she had invited me to her apartment for supper. I had the engagement ring on me and decided I had better hide it until I was ready for the grand presentation. So when dinner was ready, I slipped it under some clothing in her bedroom drawer. After eating, she went into her bedroom to change clothes for the evening's event. Pretty soon, she shouted, "What is this in my drawer?" So the proposal didn't quite work out as planned, but at least she said yes.

We went to the Catholic Church for marriage classes, another requirement for couples married in the Catholic Church. We got engaged in December of 1955 and set our wedding date for December 29, 1956. We would have married sooner, but I didn't have permission to get married until my 21st birthday. We probably would have been married on or just after my birthday, December 14, but the Catholic Church wouldn't allow us to marry during Advent. Therefore, the first Saturday available was December 29, 1956. The December 29 date had nothing to do with filing income tax forms, although a number of people assumed that had to be the reason.

5

Marriage

ON OUR WEDDING DAY, THE weather was cold and snowy. I'm sure we would have had more guests if the snow weren't so deep. The family was all there, however, and I noticed that after the marriage ceremony, my parents and Ann's mom got along great. They had done all they could to discourage us from being married, but after it was over, they no longer needed to ignore each other. The wedding, which was at 10 a.m., took place in front of the communion rails, closer to the congregation. This was because, not being a Catholic, I wasn't allowed in the sanctuary.

In those days, wedding receptions weren't very large or formal. At our reception, we served only cake, punch, nuts, and mints. It was quite the custom to open presents at the reception. We actually got rather tired of opening presents because we had so many. After finally leaving the reception hall, and before leaving on our honeymoon trip, we met at Ann's house for a light supper. We stayed that night in Scottsburg, Indiana, about thirty miles north of the Ohio River. There were no interstate highways in those days; therefore, our trip took several days. We reached Daytona Beach on New Year's Day, then drove to Tampa Bay and headed north along the Gulf of Mexico. There were few gas stations and few motels on the west coast of Florida in January 1957.

We had only $150 for our honeymoon, but we stretched it big time. Rooms averaged $6 a night, but we had so much money left over on Sunday night that we splurged on a $10 motel in Dayton, Ohio. It had an intercom system and carpeting, both of which were considered luxurious.

Our honeymoon car was a new 1956 Plymouth, a demo I received as Office Manager of Goral Motors. Even though it was such a new car, we had problems coming out of the mountains in Kentucky just a few miles south of the Ohio River across from Madison, Indiana. We had to take a taxi over the bridge into Madison; when the motel manager discovered we had no means of transportation to another motel, he increased our room price. The car problem was small, however, so it turned out not to be a big expense or inconvenience. The wedding and honeymoon didn't cost much, but were fun and exciting. The marriage has been fantastic.

6

Our Family

● ● ● ● ● ● ● ● ● ● ●

IT WAS 2 ½ YEARS before we started our family. On June 25, 1959, Ann awoke me to tell me that it was time for her to give birth to our very first child. In those days, things were just a little bit different than they are in the 21st century. First of all, the entire cost at the hospital was less than $300. Of course, since I had been born at my mom and dad's house, this was even more expensive than my birth. We also had no way of knowing whether Ann was about to give birth to a boy or girl, which was perfectly fine with us. It was rather nice being surprised, and either was going to be fantastic. The husband was not allowed in the delivery room in those days, which was terrific with me, also. I was perfectly fine with the waiting room that was set aside for expectant fathers.

When I found out that we were to go to the hospital, I was so excited that after throwing on some clothes I accidently honked my horn and backed into the side of the garage. We arrived at Parkview Hospital at about two in the morning, and Ann delivered about three in the afternoon. We had a beautiful daughter, whom we had decided to name Linda Sue.

Linda was a very good student who received mostly A's on her report card until about her freshman year in High School. Around that time, her grades took a downturn, and she didn't seem to be the same girl. Although we could see a difference in her, it took us quite a few years to discover the cause of these changes: her many allergies. As a matter of fact, we found out that she was allergic to almost everything. It was later determined that she had "Environmental Illness," a terrible disease, and Linda's life turned out to be a very difficult one.

About three years after Linda was born, Ann gave birth to Judith Ann. She was born on St. Patrick's Day, March 17, 1962. She was not only God's gift to us, but was a gift to her grandmother (my mother), who had her 52nd birthday that same day.

About three years after Judy was born, Ann gave birth to our first boy, whom we named Jeffrey James. If Judy was named Judy Ann, it was only right to make his middle name James. My busy tax season ended on April 15, 1964, and Jeff was born on April 14.

About five months later, Ann told me she was pregnant again. It was as we were headed to a family reunion that Ann made her grand announcement. The news really upset me. We were already so busy with three young children, and I wasn't getting enough time to take trips. I just thought that it was really inconsiderate of her to have another child, but I really am happy that it happened. I finally admitted that I was also responsible. We named our second son and fourth child Kenneth Wayne. Ken was born May 17, 1965 at St. Joseph Hospital in Fort Wayne, though all of our other children were born at Parkview Hospital. This was many years before Parkview relocated next to Interstate 69 in November 2010.

It would be nine years before Ann would give birth to another child, but we sure were excited when we found out she was again pregnant. I was so excited that one day I took turns telling each of the other children the good news one by one. Linda was so thrilled she let out a war whoop and ran out of the house and down the road. All of the children were really happy with the news. When it came time to tell Ken, he was really surprised and asked me if Mom knew about it. I told him, "Yes, I'm pretty sure she knows." On January 15, 1982, Ann had our fifth child, whom we named Carol Rose. Carol always liked her name, and in grade school she made the announcement that she was a flower (Rose), a song (Carol), and a bird (Seagull).

Although we were perfectly happy with five children, others also showed up on the scene every so often. One of these was Chris Hawk. Chris, a friend of Linda's, was a most discontented child. She made it known that she would like to live with us, and, in fact, did for a short time. She got involved with a cult group named "The Way." When she got married, I walked her down the aisle, something I would not have done if I knew then what "The Way" was all about.

Another was Tom Wagner, who came to live with us for a short time in about 1980. His father, a good friend of ours, had been killed in an auto accident shortly before that. Tom was about the same age as Jeff and Ken, and the three of them played a lot of table tennis during his residence with us.

On Labor Day weekend in 1981, Adam Sewards came into our "family" as a result of Jeff receiving a tip from him while a busboy at Richards Restaurant in Auburn. Usually busboys do not receive tips; Jeff, however, had gone out of his way to talk to Adam, and Adam, being a generous tipper anyways, responded by leaving a tip for Jeff with the restaurant manager. The manager gave it to Jeff, but told him that he should go over and thank this person. Adam had already left, but Jeff happened to see him again the next day and invited him to church on the following Sunday morning. When Jeff came home, he told Ann and me that some man would stop on Sunday to attend church with us. He added that the man had 37 diecast Rolls Royces. Ignoring the diecast part, we anticipated the man to be an older person, but actually he was only 20 years old at the time. Adam had a rather bad home life, and he came to really love our family. We tell others that he adopted us as parents. When Jeff went to Oral Roberts University in Tulsa, Oklahoma, it wasn't long before Adam went to Tulsa to look for a job. He got a job as a security officer for the university and later became Oral Robert's personal driver and bodyguard. Adam still thinks of us as family, and he and his many dogs visit us several times each year. He started raising Lhasa Apsos in the fall of 1985. Since we didn't want him to bring all of his dogs in the house, and yet didn't want to discourage him from visiting us, he purchased a motor home, and he really loves it.

In June 1982, a German boy named Carsten Eichart came to live with us. He was an exchange student and lived with us for about three months. We did a number of things during that summer to show him life in the United States. One was going to the Indianapolis Speedway where we all rode around the 2½-mile track. We also took him to Chicago and Niagara Falls. We required him to go to church with us every Sunday morning and every Wednesday night. He complained quite a bit about that, but I think he enjoyed most everything else that we did. Since the Amish lived close by, and since the original Amish were of German heritage, we were planning on taking him to Amish Acres on his final Sunday with us, but Adam had told him that he was taking him to Cedar Point, an Amusement Park in Sandusky, Ohio. I told Adam that we had wanted to take him to Amish Acres, and so Adam agreed to show him some Amish farm houses instead if we would allow him to take him to Cedar Point.

It turned out that Carsten found out more about Amish life with Adam than he would ever have discovered at Amish Acres. They went to a farmhouse in Grabill and made such a scene that the farmer finally asked them what they were doing there. Adam told him: "I want to show this German boy how you folks live." I could never have been that bold. However, the farmer invited them into their house and they later played volleyball with the daughters and listened to the family sing Amish songs.

Though our family continued to grow as we "adopted" new members, we knew that someday our children would leave the roost. Linda, as the oldest, was naturally the first to do so. When she was twenty-three years old, she married Ron Jacquay. Although Ron did not have a relationship with Christ when he and Linda married, he later found God and now attends Dayspring Church with us on a regular basis. Not long after their marriage, Linda gave birth to a beautiful girl, whom they named Annie (after her grandma). Linda was unable to raise Annie because of her illness, and when she was about 1½ years old, Ann and I agreed to raise her. She became our sixth child, a delightful addition to our wonderful family. As a result of her disease, Linda led a difficult life, spending several of her last years at an environmental village in Seagoville, Texas. God took her home in 2003, and she is now free from suffering. Her husband Ron continues to live with us, though. Since I was never good at any type of repair or maintenance work, Ron has been a real asset to us.

Linda on her wedding day (1982)

Ron and Linda's daughter, Annie, graduated from Huntington College in Huntington, Indiana, with a degree in education. She not only became a wonderful Christian woman, but God put on her heart to serve Christ in missions. She became aware through the Internet that she could serve Him by being a dorm mother at Rift Valley Academy in Kenya. This is a school for children of missionaries from all over the world. She served for a year in 2011 and then came back and found love. She married Taylor Chase, the son of our family doctor. He is a wonderful Christian young man, and they returned to Kenya as dorm parents in August 2013. They have since brought our first great-grandchild into the world. They named her Linda Joy, completing a four-generation cycle of passing down names (Ann had Linda, who had Annie, who had Linda). They are now expecting their second child.

Ann and I love being grandparents

Our second oldest, Judy, attended International Business College in Fort Wayne, Indiana. In 1988, she married Kim Harris, and they moved to Bronson, Michigan. Later, after having her children, she and the family moved to Bloomfield, New Mexico. After being divorced from Kim, she went back to college and graduated with an education degree from Fort Lewis College in Durango, Colorado, when she was 45 years old. They gave us two grandchildren, Miranda and Kateland (Katie). Miranda married Gabe Salazar in August 2010. Gabe and Miranda both graduated from Trinity Bible College in Ellendale, North Dakota, and they now live in Bloomfield, New Mexico. They are currently expecting their first child. Their other daughter, Katie, graduated in May 2015 from Indiana Wesleyan University in Marion, Indiana, with a degree in English and Writing. Judy and Katie moved away from New Mexico and into our house in June of 2011, which has been a wonderful blessing. Katie has since moved to Indianapolis, though, and is engaged to Alex Vernon, a godly man who fits right into the family.

Jeff attended Oral Roberts University before being led to Christ for the Nations Bible College in Dallas, Texas. He married Jennifer Bashaw in July 1988. Their wedding day particularly stands out in my memory because of what took place at the end of the wedding vows. The pastor gave the usual introduction of Jeff and Jenny now being Mr. and Mrs. Jeffrey Seigel, when unbeknownst to anyone including Jeff or the Pastor, Jenny grabbed the microphone and gave a salvation message explaining why everyone there needed to accept Jesus as Savior. Although it was a beautiful thing, it was a little unusual. It was our first occasion to assess how lovely Jenny was, and it surely cemented her acceptance into our family. Jeff served in the Army and was stationed in Frankfort, Germany. They gave us four grandchildren: Candy, Michael, Josiah, and Joy. Candy married Tyler Church in 2016, a terrific and godly young man whom God determined ought to be part of the Seigel clan. Michael has obtained his certified pastoral license, and Joy attends and plays soccer at DeKalb Middle School. Josiah's passing in 2011 was certainly sad, but we are encouraged by the thought that he is enjoying the presence of his Heavenly Father.

Josiah playing piano with Isaac

Jenny died in March 2008 from cancer and Josiah from aplastic anemia, a type of leukemia, in January 2011, a short span of time in which to lose both a wife and a son. *But God* never allowed Jeff or his family to lose faith in Him. He gave them a delightful wife and mother, Lyuba, on January 16, 2010. She came to this country from Ukraine and met Jeff while attending Emanuel Assembly in Fort Wayne. In December of 2009, Jeff asked if he could ride with us to Grabill for a wedding reception. As soon as I started driving, he told us that he was getting married the next month. As Jeff had not made any indication that he was dating or even had an interest in anyone, we were quite surprised. We became so engrossed in his story that when we reached Grabill and he still wasn't finished, we kept driving around the town to give him more time. Eventually, we even pulled into a church parking lot. Jeff had so much to share that a policeman even came up to the car to check on us. We were late to the reception, but after listening to Jeff's story, Ann and I were convinced that God had ordained this. Jeff had received assurance from God through Candy, who was attending Hillsong International Leadership College in Australia at the time. Lyuba has been a wonderful addition to the family.

Ken married Debbie Henry in May of 1989. They met at Oral Roberts University in Tulsa, Oklahoma, and both graduated from there before getting married. They gave us seven of our seventeen grandchildren: Roman, Alexander, Olivia, Julia, Arianna, Victoria, and Sophia. Roman graduated from Oral Roberts University in 2013 with a degree in accounting. Alexander graduated from Oral Roberts in 2014 with a degree in engineering. Olivia attended Oral Roberts, then transferred to Indiana-Purdue University in Fort Wayne and is pursuing a degree in music therapy. She plays the harp as well as the piano and guitar, and had the privilege in 2016 of playing the harp in the IU-PU orchestra at Carnegie Hall in New York City. Julia is currently pursuing a degree in accounting at Oral Roberts. Victoria, who has Angelman Syndrome, attends middle school in a special education class, and Arianna and Sophia attend a Christian school in Harlan, Indiana.

In December 2012, we received terrible news that Deb wanted to divorce Ken. He, as well as our entire family, is devastated, but we continue to pray that God will restore Debbie and reunite the family. It has been a lesson for our entire family of how strongly God feels about Christian marriages and how terrible divorce is in His eyes.

Carol, our youngest, married Scot Harber in May 1997. Carol graduated from Bethel College, a Christian college located in Mishawaka, Indiana. They gave us three of our grandchildren: Isaac, Sierra, and Gideon, who are homeschooled. Isaac plays basketball, Gideon loves soccer, and Sierra loves practicing piano.

Ann and I with our grandchildren (2004)

Most of our family (Christmas 2014)

Most of our grandchildren (Christmas 2015)

7

A Man Has To Work

MY FIRST JOB AFTER GRADUATION from college was Office Manager of Daily Motors in Auburn. I excelled at this job, always finishing the bookkeeping and financial statements in such a short time that I was often looking for other things to do. With my excess hours I often typed up recipes for my mom. It wasn't long before a business executive for Chrysler from Detroit observed my successes and recommended me for the position of Office Manager for Goral Motors, a much larger Chrysler Dealership on South Calhoun Street in Fort Wayne. This is where I was working at the time of my marriage.

It was in about 1960 that the owner of Goral Motors informed all of the employees that they were going to have to close the business. I was out of a job, but had a pretty good reputation as an accountant for car dealerships. Fortunately, John Ramp Lincoln Mercury, a dealership about two blocks north of Goral Motors, needed a business manager. I applied and got that job. Although it paid as well as I was paid at Goral Motors, it was much more stressful. I had never worked for a man with the personality of John Ramp. He was very firm with everyone, and it scared me. I actually started taking stress pills at age twenty-four as a result.

After working at the company for a year or two, though, I discovered that Mr. Ramp was not upset with me, but simply had the type of personality that made me think he was. I was sitting at my desk on the Friday before a vacation. Mr. Ramp came in and asked me what I was planning to do on vacation. I told him we were considering going to

Chicago, but that I didn't have the details figured out yet (which is rather unique since I usually have the details completely figured out in advance). He told me he loved Chicago and immediately called a first-class motel called "Fiftieth on The Beach." He not only paid for my family to stay there for the week, but also gave me a gift card for several restaurants. Maybe he was aware that I was nervous around him and wanted to keep me. However, in January 1961, he also had to close his business.

After losing two jobs at car dealerships to bankruptcy, I figured I had better find a job in some other industry. Unfortunately, there weren't many jobs available. Thankfully, I knew I had lost both jobs due to the recession, not incompetency, and should be able to find a job eventually. Ann was not employed; she was a housewife, a job with lots of work but no financial compensation. Reluctantly, I agreed to let her go to work until I could find a job. She had worked as a secretary at Central Soya after college until Linda was born and was fully competent, holding the record for speed typing at International College, at least at that time. So she took a job at Magnavox to support us until I could find a job.

But God knew our situation and had a career in store for me that I never would have come up with on my own. I placed my application at an employment agency. In March, after being out of work for about two months, my big break came. Herb Cooper, a certified public accountant, was the senior partner in an accounting firm called Cooper, Brandt, and Brunner (the name later expanded to six names with eleven partners). Although I had never had experience in public accounting and never applied as a CPA, he thought I would qualify because I had done bookkeeping at auto dealerships, which had a reputation for having the most complicated bookkeeping system there is. I had never considered getting into public accounting, but I was so flattered with his interest in me that I accepted the job.

A blessing took place at this job that basically changed my whole career. On New Year's Day of 1964, the day before my first tax season began, Herb Cooper was ice-skating and broke his right wrist. He would not be able to write just as tax and audit season was about to begin. At first, this seemed like it would be disastrous, *but God* proved His faithfulness even in this. Mr. Cooper decided that since I was the new kid on the block, he would take me with him wherever he went. I could work the adding machine and do the writing while he could supply the brainpower. That would get him through the season, and it proved to be an invaluable help for me. I really learned a lot that year. I liked my job and decided to study for the CPA examination. It is a very detailed exam with four parts. In those days passing the exam and having a two-year degree qualified someone to become a CPA. Today I would need a five-year degree. I managed to get my CPA certificate by passing Accounting and Tax, followed by passing Auditing and finally Business Law.

In the fall of 1967, I was made the eleventh and final partner of the firm. Later, I persuaded the other partners to allow me to open an office in Auburn, my hometown. Not only were there no CPA offices in Auburn, but there weren't any in all of DeKalb County. This turned out to be a great opportunity to grow an accounting business. Normally, a person trying to begin a new business has trouble making an income while getting established and getting clients, *but God* once again worked His will in my life. I was able to work on jobs for the other partners while receiving my own clientele.

I opened an upstairs office above Attorney Phyllis Poff's office on Fifth and Cedar in Auburn, which worked out nicely. Her secretary answered phone calls and took messages for me when I worked in the Fort Wayne office (which was in the Anthony Wayne Bank building). Our partnership was a little unique in that we did not share net income; instead, we shared expenses based on the hours in our personal ledgers, which meant that every new account I got increased only my individual income. My personal business grew quite rapidly. One of the reasons, other than hardly any competition, was that there was a lady in the area who prepared a lot of income taxes. Nearly all of the returns she prepared were wrong, and the great majority of them favored the government. When people brought their returns to me to examine I was able to get them rather large refunds. That kind of news spread fast and gave me a reputation as an excellent tax preparer; the truth was this lady did such a bad job it made me look good.

Rance Buehrer had an office in Angola, I had the office in Auburn, and the other nine partners had the office in Fort Wayne. The Fort Wayne practice was quite different in that it was primarily an audit practice while the Auburn and Angola offices were primarily tax. Because of this, any partnership decisions were usually 9-2. As a result, Rance and I decided to leave the firm, and in 1978, we retained our separate offices under a new partnership name, Buehrer and Seigel. Cooper, Brandt, and Brunner wrote a letter to all my clients telling them that I was leaving the Partnership and that they should respond to the letter what they were going to do. They could transfer to Buehrer and Seigel or they could continue with the Fort Wayne office with a different accountant. Over 90% percent transferred to me. By this time I had moved to a new location at 116 W. Sixth Street. After several years, Buehrer and I agreed to each have a separate practice.

Business went well; before long my firm needed more space, so I purchased the building I was in, as well as the building next door, and remodeled the entire space into one rather large office building. I now had Steve Seigel, my nephew, and Pat Hart, a very qualified accountant, working for me. Both of them were CPAs. Quite interesting is that Steve had become an accountant because of advice I had given him many years earlier. He had been a cook at Richard's Restaurant in Auburn and wasn't sure what he would do in life. I suggested that he consider becoming a CPA, so he did. I made both Pat and Steve partners, and we named the firm "The Seigel Group."

Even with a larger staff, though, we encountered challenging projects during the summer of 1991 that made me realize that I needed still more help. *But God* came to the rescue. Ken, my fourth-born, had told me a number of times that he had no interest in ever coming to Auburn. This was never a problem for me, since I never had any expectations of him working for me. He called me at home one July evening, and when he found out I was working even though it wasn't the tax season, he was quite surprised. I told him how busy I was right then and added as an afterthought, "I sure wish you were here." I didn't even realize what I had said; it just came out. Several nights later, Ken called again and, on finding me at the office again, he asked, "Dad, did you really mean what you said?" I replied, "What did I say?" He said, "You said you wished I were there. If you mean that, I think I might consider it."

This really came as a shock to me, because I wasn't sure I could use him full time. The present circumstance was an unusual event, not the norm. I didn't want to hire Ken unless I knew I could keep him busy all of the time, because I knew he wouldn't be happy otherwise. After a number of interviews, I made the decision that I would hire him even if I had to give him all of the work that I would normally do. It was a great decision. He did such good work that our firm's business grew to the point that both he and I were busy. He was really good at auditing but had very little tax knowledge. Our firm was very good at preparing taxes, but not qualified to do audits. We taught him taxes, and he taught us auditing.

As the business continued, I made the decision to make Ken a partner also. We were very successful and earned a good name in our community. On December 31, 1995, I sold my practice to the other 3 partners over a five-year period, and on December 31, 2000, I retired at the age of 65. I had really enjoyed my life as an accountant, but I was ready for retirement. As it turned out, I wasn't finished preparing income taxes. My primary clients simply became seniors and low-income people at the senior center in Auburn, where I have volunteered every tax season for the past eight years.

8

Where We Lived

IN THE MONTH PRECEDING OUR marriage, Ann and I began looking at various rental properties. We found half of a duplex on Packard Avenue in the southwest part of Fort Wayne that we both agreed was better than any of the apartments we had looked at. We had also purchased furniture so that when we returned from our honeymoon, we could immediately have a place to live. Once again, it was a Chrysler field rep who played an important part in our lives. When we discovered that Ann was pregnant with Linda in September of 1959, we realized that we would need a bigger place. I wasn't sure that we could afford to purchase a house. We had viewed a house that had just been built in Concordia Gardens, a housing addition north of Concordia College on the north side of Fort Wayne. When I discussed this with my boss and the Chrysler representative from Detroit, they both stated that my job status was really good, and they recommended that we purchase it. It cost around $18,000, and that seemed like an awful lot of money to me. Looking back now, it would seem $18,000 wasn't a lot of money, but this was new territory for us. Ann and I purchased it, and were the first occupants of the house at 2313 Belleview Drive, which turned out to be a good place to begin raising a family. We lived there from December 1958 until December 1969. We had four of our five children while we lived on Belleview Drive, at which point we decided it was time for a larger and nicer house.

We located a beautiful house in Northcrest Woods just a block south of Washington Center Road in Fort Wayne (5725 Dartmouth Drive). We both really liked this house, but of course we would need to sell the one on Belleview Drive before we could purchase it. Ken Wolff was a high school friend who graduated with me. We decided to invite him and Charlotte, his wife, over, and they agreed to allow me to practice a sales approach on them. I must have done a pretty good job, because they decided to buy the house from us, which then enabled us to close on the Dartmouth Drive property. We moved on December 19, 1969, just before Christmas. Even after a heavy day of moving, I still set up the outdoor Christmas lights that same evening. I really loved this house and thought it would be ours forever. It was large, beautiful in our minds, and was in a good location. It had four large upstairs bedrooms, two baths, a gigantic living room, dining room, large breakfast area, a two-car garage, and a nice family room. We even loved the location, except that I had to drive to Auburn every day to work. We were certainly not looking to relocate anywhere.

9

Buying Our Farm

● ● ● ● ● ● ● ● ● ● ●

In January of 1976, I was reading the Sunday Journal-Gazette one day when I took notice of a four-page advertisement telling about a real estate auction held by Kruse Realtors. Although none of my family members had ever discussed moving, I took special interest in the ad for a couple of reasons. First, I knew and respected Dean and Dennis Kruse, who were the auctioneers. Second, the two featured properties meant something to me. The first was a motel in Angola named Redwood Motel. This motel was right across the Highway from my Angola office. I had eaten at the motel restaurant quite often. (Quite interestingly, this motel had a fire, and years later was sold to my son Jeff, who later sold it to Ken and I—but that is a completely different story). The other featured property the ad called "One of DeKalb County's Finest Country Estates." It showed pictures of a house and barn, which, together with the magnificent descriptions the advertisement mentioned, made me quite certain that this property was the Rieke Estate on the south edge of Auburn. I had passed that property many times going or returning from my Auburn accounting office and was curious to see it.

The next day I was in my Auburn office, and I decided to call Dean Kruse, who I knew fairly well. I said, "Dean, I see that the Reike Mansion is for sale." He replied, "No, what do you mean?" I told him that I was referring to the advertisement in the Fort Wayne Journal Gazette. "Oh!" he replied. "That property's on County Road 19." Although I had lived nearly my whole life in Auburn, I had no idea where County Road 19 was. I was just never acquainted with the farming areas. So I told him thanks for the information and admitted that I had only been curious; I merely wanted to view the Rieke property and get an idea about what it was worth.

Dean got excited, however, and said he wondered why he hadn't thought about me in the first place. He said that since I was an Auburn businessman with five children, it would be an ideal place for me to live. We would not only have a large house, but also seventy acres of land for the children to play. I reminded him that I had no desire to move, that we owned a lovely, fairly large, home in Fort Wayne, and the short drive was not a problem. "Thanks, anyway," I replied. He answered, "Why not look at it anyhow, since you noticed it in the paper?" Eventually, Dean persuaded me to view the property.

Although the only reason I even viewed the property was because of Dean's persuasion, I surprised myself and liked it. I knew that I had never had any inclinations for farming, but I realized what a great place it would be for the kids, and I knew that I would be able to rent the land out. The person who had owned the property was a Corporate Executive at Reike Corporation, and he wasn't a farmer. I could even see that the land and buildings had income potential. I liked all of the outbuildings, the extra home that already had a tenant, and the basement. We had never had a basement.

Ann was able to discern my excitement about the property and asked me to see if she and the kids could see it too. Dean was only too happy to show it again. The children loved it, and Ann liked it enough that we discussed it. It would be a nice place, but could we afford it? Since it was to be sold at a real estate auction, there was no asking price listed. I didn't know what a farmhouse with seventy acres of land, plus a rental house, several buildings, and a large barn, was worth, and there really weren't any similar farms on the market to compare it to at the time. We did what we often did in an important matter, though—we prayed. "Lord," we asked, "are we really supposed to take an interest in this property? Should we go to the real estate auction?" The auction was held in a large conference room in Fort Wayne on a Saturday morning in March 1976. This was tax season. I wondered if I should be taking a Saturday off just out of curiosity, especially since I had no complaints with the lovely home

God had already provided for us. I didn't do much research because I didn't know where to do so or if I was even really interested. I knew my interest was increasing, though, since we had already made several trips by the property.

Just a few days prior to the auction day, the Lord let me know that I was to bid $125,000 for the property. That was within the boundaries I could afford, but I didn't know where this thought had come from. I hadn't dreamt it, and God hadn't made an appearance that I could detect but I felt sure the direction was from the Lord. Anyway, with this in mind, Ann and I went to the auction. The Kruse brothers showed pictures on the screen and had sold many properties before the Auburn "Estate" came up. With little fanfare, bids came fast and furious. I hardly had a chance to bid, but finally got in a bid of $125,000, exactly the price I had heard in my mind just days before.

The next thing that happened is still unexplainable to this day. Dean and Dennis Kruse are truly professional in every way, and after my bid, even without any letup or slowing down in the bidding, Dean stopped to say more about this fabulous estate. Normally, when the bidding is fast and furious the auctioneer continues without interruption, but Dean paused to show dozens of pictures of everything the farm had to offer, including every angle of the main house, the rental house, and various views of the barn, the silo, the rental house, and the outbuildings. I later heard that Fred Quance, who was selling the property, almost changed his mind because Dean made it sound so lovely. I leaned over to Ann, and in a moment of faithlessness made the comment, "Look how fast the bids came in before this sales pitch. I don't have a chance now, for sure." *But God* wanted Ann and I to have this place. The bidding had ceased at $125,000, and now Dean explained he would take additional bids. I had to decide what I would do when bids started to come again. If it was God who gave me the amount to bid, should I bid more? I never had to answer that, though, because, miraculously and unexplainably, no additional bids ever took place. Where there had been no letup in bids prior to that superb job of salesmanship, now there were no additional bids.

A problem soon arose, however. Although I had made the highest bid, this type of auction gave the right of refusal to the seller. So after the sale, Fred Quance met with Dean and Ann and I to discuss the situation.

Fred was extremely disappointed with the bidding, having expected much more for the property. I explained that I had bid the amount I felt appropriate, and didn't think I should increase the amount. I didn't have the nerve to explain that God had told me how much to bid; I am sure he wouldn't have accepted that explanation anyway. Finally, I reluctantly agreed to $140,000, on the terms that I would not be required to buy if my Fort Wayne property didn't sell. *But God* again intervened. I also agreed to pay him $25,000 on April 30, another $25,000 on June 30, and the remaining $90,000 at a September 30 closing. On April 15, Fred called me and said that if I would pay the April payment immediately, he would reduce the price by $5,000. On May 15, he called me again and said he needed more money, and that if I paid the May payment, he would reduce the price another $5,000. On the day of closing, I had not sold my Fort Wayne property yet; it looked like the sale wouldn't be closed. I did have a tentative buyer, though, who didn't want to pay as much as I was asking for my house. As a result, I told Fred that if he would reduce the price by another $5,000, I would approve the Fort Wayne sale and close on the Auburn property. He agreed to this, thus making the final reduced price $125,000, the original price God had put into my mind.

We often asked why God wanted us on the farm, but within a couple of months of living there, we found out that Jeff and Ken had started hanging out with the wrong crowd and were in danger of getting into trouble. We are convinced that we had found out why God arranged this whole thing. Since then, we have praised God numerous times for allowing us to buy the farm. It has been a wonderful atmosphere, a good investment, and later, after selling several acres to Jeff, we were able to have our son and his family as neighbors. We rented out what we thought was 63.5 acres until 2008, when we sold 67.9 acres. God had given us about 4.5 acres more than we thought we had originally purchased. We received $225,000 for the land, $100,000 more than we had paid for the entire property, and Jeff and I still own 5.5 acres, plus I still own the house and the buildings.

We love croquet so much we even play in December! (2015)

The Flag on our Barn

When Jeff returned from serving in Saudi Arabia in 1991, I had the wild idea to have the United States flag painted on four 4'x8' boards (together making a 8'x16' flag), which we then mounted on the south side of our barn. The family liked the idea, and the story made the local

Our House

Over the years we have grown to love the farm for mar
didn't anticipate at first. We love the fact that County Roa
and easy to travel, yet very quiet. We love having our son,
family living next door, and we like being rather secluded. A
loves all the privacy we have, and that there is no need to
people looking in or keeping the blinds closed. We have ple
to get together with the family. We have even been able to
potlucks and playing Frisbee or croquet in our spacious yard.
family is really competitive, playing many vigorous games o
family favorite. The barn and land we still have provides a
and Michael to have two horses. We were even able to provide
setting for Judy's wedding.

We love croquet so much we even play in December! (2015)

The Flag on our Barn

When Jeff returned from serving in Saudi Arabia in 1991, I had the wild idea to have the United States flag painted on four 4'x8' boards (together making a 8'x16' flag), which we then mounted on the south side of our barn. The family liked the idea, and the story made the local

Our House

Over the years we have grown to love the farm for many reasons we didn't anticipate at first. We love the fact that County Road 19 is paved and easy to travel, yet very quiet. We love having our son, Jeff, and his family living next door, and we like being rather secluded. Ann especially loves all the privacy we have, and that there is no need to worry about people looking in or keeping the blinds closed. We have plenty of room to get together with the family. We have even been able to host church potlucks and playing Frisbee or croquet in our spacious yard. In fact, our family is really competitive, playing many vigorous games of croquet, a family favorite. The barn and land we still have provides a way for Jeff and Michael to have two horses. We were even able to provide a beautiful setting for Judy's wedding.

newspaper and even the annual county report cover. The flag is visible to anyone traveling north on County Road 19.

Ann and I realized at age 75 that maybe taking care of this large house and yard was too much for us. We went so far as to put a deposit on a smaller apartment by Walmart in Auburn. *But God* had other plans for us. When our kids and grandkids found out about this, they were really upset. We had never realized that our family loved the farm so much. In fact, it was then that we found out they were even disappointed that we had sold off the excess acreage. All of the kids and grandkids really love the farm.

About the same time that we were planning on selling our property and moving to the apartment, Judy and Katie told us that they were planning to move back to Auburn in June of 2011. When Annie heard that we might sell our house, she informed us of something we were never aware of. She told us that Judy and Katie would like to live with us, which would mean Ann would have help in maintaining the house. And when we called Judy to verify, she said it was indeed true. We fixed up a couple of rooms upstairs so they could have their own apartment, and everything turned out wonderfully. Now, Katie lives in Indianapolis, but for a while, we had our son-in-law, daughter, and granddaughter all living with us. Judy insists on doing most of the cooking and cleaning, and Ron does most of the maintenance. How blessed we are. The place would undoubtedly be terribly unkempt if it were not for Ron and Judy.

10

Health Issues

OTHER THAN BEING BORN WITH only one working eye, I had very few health issues until retirement. Having only one eye has never been a real problem for me, since God made up for it by giving me more peripheral vision in my left eye. I had been in the hospital only once in my life—for a hemorrhoid operation when I was in my late twenties—and very seldom even needed to see a doctor. In January of 2001, less than a month after retiring, I experienced some pain in my neck. I was somewhat concerned, so I agreed to go to my doctor. After a cursory examination, my doctor suggested I see Dr. Genetos, a heart doctor in Fort Wayne, who ran a scope of my heart and determined that I had blockage and would need surgery. I explained that we were about to leave on a trip to Hawaii, and he determined that I would be able to take that trip before having further medical procedures, but that I should have bypass surgery when I returned. It turned out that I only required a double bypass, which I had soon after returning home from that trip.

My new relationship with doctors and hospitals didn't end there, however. On June 9, 2001, I was mowing the lawn with a riding mower when the somewhat wet grass was clogging up the mower. Thinking that I had turned off the blades, I reached in to clear out the clogged grass only to discover that the mower blades had not stopped. My thumb and half of my index finger were severed immediately from my right hand. Although I was probably 150 yards from the house, I somehow managed to cross the distance and make it inside. Ann called an ambulance to take me to

42

Parkview Hospital, but because of my recent bypass surgery, I was not allowed to have any painkillers. Thankfully, I had already taken one pain tablet before they told me this, but I could have used a few more. I had never experienced such pain before, and it seemed like hours before the ambulance left for the hospital. Fortunately, a hand surgeon was available when we arrived at Parkview. Although they were not able to save the finger and thumb, the surgical team did a super job of sewing me up.

It's funny how one small mistake can change a person's life. I learned pretty quickly how important a couple of fingers could be. While recovering from surgery, I attempted to learn how to write left-handed, but failed completely. I consoled myself with the fact that at least the accident hadn't happened until my retirement, so I didn't have to do nearly as much writing. Once my right hand healed, I had to relearn how to write without a finger or thumb, and previously simple tasks, such as shuffling cards or opening jars, were much more difficult. In fact, I have never been able to successfully button my left shirtsleeve since the incident. Ann has to do it for me. Eventually, though, I was able to conquer most daily tasks, and now I get along pretty well.

I didn't have many other health issues until 2007, when I learned that I have diverticulosis. As a result, I now get a colonoscopy every couple of years. Although the doctors have found polyps with each colonoscopy, none of them have appeared cancerous. Ann and I began a gluten-free diet when I received this diagnosis, and though it was difficult to adjust to at first, we have since adapted. In fact, I think our diet causes more problems for the friends and family that we dine with than it does for us. As if this major change in our lives wasn't enough, I also had a heart attack in 2007. This time, I didn't need a bypass, only stents. It was on this occasion that Sue Lyne, our pastor's wife, left her shift at DeKalb Hospital to ride with me to Parkview Hospital. My heart stopped twice that night—once inside DeKalb Hospital and again in the ambulance just before it left for Parkview.

My weakened heart has slowed me down considerably ever since, and my family now makes sure that I don't overextend myself. I now have a pacemaker and a defibrillator. My heart attack proved that after nearly sixty years of marriage, Ann and I do almost everything together. Not only did she join me in my gluten-free diet, but she also had a heart attack less than a month after I had mine. We both recovered, however.

In April 2015, I inexplicably began to cough a lot. I just kept getting worse and sometimes would continue until it really wore me out. Although I made several appointments with Dr. Chase, he was unable to figure out what the trouble was. Finally, in October, after six months of coughing, he sent me to Dr. Ghanem, a pulmonologist. Almost immediately, he was able to determine that I had pulmonary fibrosis of the lungs. Although this is incurable, he has prescribed various procedures that keep me fairly comfortable, including a much better CPAP sleep machine. For taking a vast number of pills each day, I feel pretty good while I write this during my eightieth year on earth. God is good.

11

Unique Occasions

SEVERAL YEARS AFTER I ENTERED retirement, an unusual situation occurred with Dick and Mary Lou Ripberger, good friends of ours. Although they lived about 100 miles from us, Ann and I had been to their house a number of times for visits. They were a wonderful couple, and had so much in common with us. They had five children, as do we, and Mary Lou was even born on the very same day I was, in the same year. Distance made our visits much too infrequent, so when I got the opportunity to visit, I became quite excited. While I was their C.P.A., prior to retirement, I had recommended a number of times that they do some estate planning. Richard, however, had never expressed any interest in doing this. So when Mary Lou called and asked me to come meet with them, their daughter, and their attorney to do some estate planning, I was pleased. Not only was I happy that they had called on me, even though I had been retired for several years, but I was also looking forward to the possibility of sharing fellowship and a meal with them after the business discussion. Thus, I suggested to the Ripbergers that I bring Ann with me. She could relax in the family room while we talked business, and then we could all go to a restaurant after the meeting concluded. They thought this was a good idea, so we made our plans.

We were to arrive at their home at noon so their attorney and their daughter, who was also their bookkeeper, could both meet with us. Their daughter needed to return home by 3 p.m. to relieve her babysitter, so Ann and I paid particular attention to the clock and were careful to arrive at their house several minutes before noon, when the meeting was to start. As we pulled up, though, we noticed that no cars were parked in the driveway. This seemed odd, since they had put emphasis on starting the meeting on time. The Ripbergers had a lovely home in the country, several miles from the town their attorney was from, so I decided that my best option was to use their telephone to contact them. I knew this would be all right with them, since we were longtime friends and had been to this home a number of times. Besides, the back door was unlocked, and I knew they wanted me at the meeting.

I had a surprisingly hard time finding their telephone. After searching for a couple of minutes, I finally located one in the bedroom, with a phone book in the nightstand where it sat. Calling the attorney, however, did no good. The answering machine merely informed me that the office was closed from noon to 1. Remembering that I had the daughter's phone number in my briefcase, I hurried to my car and brought the briefcase in. Spreading the files on the dining room table, I found the daughter's number. Her aunt answered the phone, and was surprised to hear of my dilemma. She said that this indeed was the right day and time, and that the meeting should be taking place even as we talked. She thought for several moments and then said, "You do know that they moved several months ago, don't you?"

At that moment I realized I was sitting in a stranger's bedroom talking long-distance on their telephone. Mary Lou had obviously thought I was aware of their move, but had never actually informed me. In any event, as soon as I could get directions to the Ripbergers' new residence, I was getting out of there as quickly as possible. The aunt gave me their new phone number, and I quickly made the call to get directions to the new house and explain why I had not yet arrived. Apparently, the Ripbergers had sent me a note informing me of their move when I prepared their tax return, but when I reviewed the return, I hadn't even noticed that another accountant working for me at the time had changed the address on file.

All of this time, Ann had been waiting in the car to avoid being jumped on by the rather large dog, as I had been when first entering the porch. We hurried to the meeting, and although I was forty-five minutes late, I was able to catch up on the discussions. The meeting had been handled very well, even concluding on time so that their daughter could return home. Several times during the meeting, however, I was unable to find a specific file folder to confirm some of my comments. After the meeting, the Ripbergers, Ann, and I had a wonderful time at a restaurant in Kokomo catching up and laughing about why I had been late for the meeting.

Many hours later, on the way back to Auburn, I suddenly realized where the missing file folder was. In my haste to leave that house, I had left the file folder on the dining room table. I hated to admit what I had done, especially to the homeowners, but I reluctantly agreed with Ann that I needed to go back to the house to get the file. It contained many confidential items that surely shouldn't be in some stranger's house. When we arrived, the new homeowner was busy playing with his dog, which, although quite large, was really still a puppy. When the dog didn't seem alarmed at my presence, I explained to the owner that I was already acquainted with his dog, and then reluctantly shared what had taken place earlier in the day.

Apparently, since I was dressed in a suit and tie, and because I knew the Ripbergers by name, the man believed my story. He was headed inside to get the file for me, but then paused and said, "Why don't you go get the file yourself? You know where everything is, anyway." The whole story could have turned out much worse, and while it was stressful at the time, everything really turned out quite well. No one had gone inside the house yet, and the contents of that file remained confidential.

Another event that Ann still chuckles about happened on a cold winter night in 1967. I attended a church meeting that evening at Gethsemane Lutheran Church. After the meeting, I put on my overcoat to leave, but as I was leaving the church, someone stopped to talk. After talking with him for some time, I put on my overcoat and went home. I went into my Concordia Garden house and took off my overcoat and put it in the hall closet. When I entered the kitchen I discovered that I still had my overcoat on. I was sure that I had taken it off, and sure enough, when I checked the hall closet there it was. It really was true that I had worn two overcoats when returning from the meeting. It was then that I remembered my conversation at church where I had put on my overcoat, and remembered that I had already put one on prior to my discussion. I hurried back to the church, and am pretty sure that whomever the larger coat belonged to had not yet left the church. I could later laugh about this, but had problems admitting to it at first.

Another of my wife's favorite stories about me took place at the beach in North Carolina. Ken had invited us to spend a week with his family at a beautiful house there; Ann and I had arrived before Ken's family while the house was still being readied for our week's stay. We were allowed to sit in the pool area while we waited for Ken and the family to arrive, so we were both spending the time reading. I was really involved with my book, apparently, because when I heard someone drive up I got up to look out the back and see if Ken had arrived. I proceeded to walk right into the pool, clothing and all. Fortunately, it was the shallow end and I was not hurt. However the book and I were both soaked. Ann had to get me a change of clothes and had my billfold contents spread out all over the place to dry when Ken entered the house.

One unique occasion I often think about occurred during my daughter-in-law Jenny's funeral. Jenny had a reputation not only for being close to Jesus, but also for being late to almost everything. While everyone was waiting to follow the hearse to the cemetery, we discovered that the hearse had, in fact, broken down, and we would have to wait quite a long time for another one. Those who knew her found it amusing that Jenny was late to even her own funeral.

Ann and I decided to plan our own funerals some years ago, a process which included choosing out own monument and gravesite, choosing the songs that will be played during the service, and paying for everything in advance. We did so in order to save our children the pain and cost of doing it themselves. Something laughable happened when our headstones were being made, though. Some dear friends of ours, Jim and Pat Ankney, drove past the monument company and were really quite concerned when they saw our names inscribed on a stone outside. They called our house to make sure we were okay, and we convinced them that we were.

Another cute story (at least others seem to find it so) took place when I was eighty years old. I was at home and kept hearing a loud buzzing sound. I tried and tried to determine what it could be and prayed that it wasn't anything serious taking place in our house. Ron and I both searched every room, because we could hear the buzzing sound no matter where we looked. When Ron went into the next room, though, he reported that the noise disappeared. When I followed him into a room, however, I could still hear the noise. Finally, we discovered that my cell phone, which I frequently carry but rarely use, had a radio on it that had accidentally been turned on and was creating the buzzing noise.

Ann and I were both seventy-eight when this next story took place. Our granddaughter, who was thirty-two at this time, is named Anne after my wife, but goes by "Annie." In August of 2013, Annie went on a mission trip to Kenya with her husband, Taylor. Their mission was to be dorm parents for the children of missionaries at Rift Valley Academy, a school for the children of missionaries serving in Africa.

In September, an acquaintance saw me at her garage sale and asked me how Annie was. So I responded that Annie was just fine, and added that she had just left for a four-year mission trip to Africa. I could tell that she was quite startled by that but didn't know why until she explained that she was asking about my wife, not my granddaughter. For some reason, she had always thought that my wife's name was Annie. She obviously felt that it was quite inconsiderate of me to let my wife move thousands of miles from me, even if it was for a good cause.

A year later I saw this lady again, without immediately remembering the incident at her garage sale. Again, she asked me how Annie was. I had just been notified that Annie was pregnant with my first great-grandchild, so I proudly responded that Annie was great and, in fact, was now pregnant. Knowing that Ann and I were quite elderly, I believe the lady nearly fainted.

12

Travel

ANN AND I HAVE ALWAYS been blessed with the ability to travel frequently. Because I really love to travel, much of my finances and time have gone for travel. Before the kids left home, we had a vacation nearly every summer that included some travel. Some of the most memorable places we vacationed to were Florida (a number of times), the northeastern states to view the fall colors, Cape Cod, all parts of Michigan, Kentucky, Chicago and other parts of Illinois, Alaska, St. Louis and other parts of Missouri, and even, incredibly, Colorado (a trip of over 3,000 miles without air conditioning, as it was not standard car equipment in those years). In addition, we have traveled to England, Scotland, Australia, New Zealand, Germany, Austria, Switzerland, Norway, Denmark, Finland, and several islands while cruising, including our first Atlantic trip in 1970 to Jamaica. One year Ann and I even went to Stratford, Canada, a beautiful city that was modeled after Stratford, England. Although we originally intended to watch a Shakespearian play, we instead decided to attend a number of Chamber Orchestra Concerts, which is where we began our love for classical music.

Just north of Mackinaw is a beautiful state park called Tahquamenon Falls. Our kids had lots of fun crossing a shallow stream with a floating log, which seemed to scream, "Cross over on me!" The log was wet and slippery, and Judy fell right in. Despite her being cold and wet for a while, we all had a big laugh, Judy included. Later, when we were in Charlevoix, we stopped at a roadside picnic area to eat our lunch. I had seen all of the poisoning. The bathroom was in almost constant use for the rest of the night. We had to get to the airport that next morning for our flight back to Detroit. Jeff had planned to take us to the airport, but now that was impossible. Neither Jenny nor any of us had a license to drive in Germany. Finally Jeff relented and called his pastor. Our plane was going to leave shortly, and we were sure we would miss the flight. Germany has outside lanes, called the Autobahn, that have no speed limit. Jeff's pastor decided that driving in these lanes was the only way to make it to the airport on time, so we raced down them at some of the fastest speeds I have ever traveled. Our stomachs weren't thanking us, but we made it to the airport just in time to board our flight. We were so late, though, that the only seats remaining were scattered in different parts of the plane. I usually love flying, but that trip from Frankfort, Germany to Detroit was no fun.

But God had known our plight and had already determined what would happen next. Before we left for our trip, Adam had insisted on picking us up in Detroit when we returned from Germany and taking us back to Auburn. At the time, we had tried to tell him this was foolish, since we could save him time simply by driving ourselves. But now we were so sick it turned out we really did need him. God truly supplies in every need, even when we think His plans make no sense at first.

In 1998, I was able to cross off one of the trips that was always on my bucket list. I grew up loving flowers. My mom would always watch the Rose Parade on New Year's Day. She loved flowers, and they were beautiful to her even on black-and-white TV. Watching the parade in color every New Year's Day has been my tradition for over 50 years, so seeing it in person was truly remarkable.

One of the unique aspects of many of our trips was staying in people's homes. We had heard about "Mennonite Your Way," a booklet that listed Mennonite families who welcomed guests into their homes for a small fee. Originally, we did this to save money, since a night's lodging cost only $8 per person; after our first experience, though, we discovered that we rather enjoyed the people, the fellowship, and their suggestions for sites and activities.

Although Ann and I have been to many places, one trip we had never taken was to see New York City. We discovered that Carol's mother-in-law, Charlene, had a brother and sister-in-law who lived in Brooklyn. She had

kids in the back of the van and didn't realize that Judy had
make room for the cooler. When I took off, the kids hollered
had been left behind. This made me a little angry because I k
in the back, so I responded that I didn't think this was at al
children persisted that she had indeed been left behind, and
when I looked out the back I saw her running after us as fast
legs could carry her. After these two episodes, we're glad she s

In 1988, we visited Germany, Switzerland, Lichtenstein,
At the time, Jeff was stationed in Germany with the Army,
Jenny had arranged a fabulous vacation trip for our family
them. Although we really enjoyed the entire trip, the highlig
us had to be the tour of The Sound of Music filming location
us to see some beautiful scenery from a movie that we loved
the church where Maria and Georg von Trapp were married, t
the street where the von Trapp children went tree climbing, a
where the family fell out of the boat. This opportunity made us
the movie even more.

One of the things I especially remember about this trip is
that Jeff had. It was an old Volkswagen van, and we cramme
into it (Jeff, Jenny, Ken, Carol, Ann, and I). In addition to the
six passengers and our luggage, we also had taken a little refrig
lots of food. We traveled on a lot of mountainous roads, and tha
van could barely make it up them, weighed down as it was.
though, it managed to get us where we needed to go.

The day before we returned home, Jenny wanted to make us
meal. We couldn't find an open grocery store anywhere, though.
was holding their annual wine festival, and all German busine
closed for the occasion. The army normally would have had some
px stores open (post exchange shops made available for Army
stationed in Germany), but that day they were also closed becau
Columbus Day in the United States. After running out of other
Jenny remembered that she had the ingredients to make a fav
recipe for us.

We later learned that Germany has a policy of leavi
unrefrigerated. Apparently, these were purchased at a German
store, because that evening everyone in the house got sick wi

poisoning. The bathroom was in almost constant use for the rest of the night. We had to get to the airport that next morning for our flight back to Detroit. Jeff had planned to take us to the airport, but now that was impossible. Neither Jenny nor any of us had a license to drive in Germany. Finally Jeff relented and called his pastor. Our plane was going to leave shortly, and we were sure we would miss the flight. Germany has outside lanes, called the Autobahn, that have no speed limit. Jeff's pastor decided that driving in these lanes was the only way to make it to the airport on time, so we raced down them at some of the fastest speeds I have ever traveled. Our stomachs weren't thanking us, but we made it to the airport just in time to board our flight. We were so late, though, that the only seats remaining were scattered in different parts of the plane. I usually love flying, but that trip from Frankfort, Germany to Detroit was no fun.

But God had known our plight and had already determined what would happen next. Before we left for our trip, Adam had insisted on picking us up in Detroit when we returned from Germany and taking us back to Auburn. At the time, we had tried to tell him this was foolish, since we could save him time simply by driving ourselves. But now we were so sick it turned out we really did need him. God truly supplies in every need, even when we think His plans make no sense at first.

In 1998, I was able to cross off one of the trips that was always on my bucket list. I grew up loving flowers. My mom would always watch the Rose Parade on New Year's Day. She loved flowers, and they were beautiful to her even on black-and-white TV. Watching the parade in color every New Year's Day has been my tradition for over 50 years, so seeing it in person was truly remarkable.

One of the unique aspects of many of our trips was staying in people's homes. We had heard about "Mennonite Your Way," a booklet that listed Mennonite families who welcomed guests into their homes for a small fee. Originally, we did this to save money, since a night's lodging cost only $8 per person; after our first experience, though, we discovered that we rather enjoyed the people, the fellowship, and their suggestions for sites and activities.

Although Ann and I have been to many places, one trip we had never taken was to see New York City. We discovered that Carol's mother-in-law, Charlene, had a brother and sister-in-law who lived in Brooklyn. She had kids in the back of the van and didn't realize that Judy had gotten out to make room for the cooler. When I took off, the kids hollered out that Judy had been left behind. This made me a little angry because I knew she was in the back, so I responded that I didn't think this was at all funny. The children persisted that she had indeed been left behind, and sure enough, when I looked out the back I saw her running after us as fast as her little legs could carry her. After these two episodes, we're glad she still loved us.

In 1988, we visited Germany, Switzerland, Lichtenstein, and Austria. At the time, Jeff was stationed in Germany with the Army, and he and Jenny had arranged a fabulous vacation trip for our family to come see them. Although we really enjoyed the entire trip, the highlight for all of us had to be the tour of The Sound of Music filming locations. It enabled us to see some beautiful scenery from a movie that we loved, including the church where Maria and Georg von Trapp were married, the convent, the street where the von Trapp children went tree climbing, and the lake where the family fell out of the boat. This opportunity made us appreciate the movie even more.

One of the things I especially remember about this trip is the vehicle that Jeff had. It was an old Volkswagen van, and we crammed six of us into it (Jeff, Jenny, Ken, Carol, Ann, and I). In addition to the weight of six passengers and our luggage, we also had taken a little refrigerator and lots of food. We traveled on a lot of mountainous roads, and that little old van could barely make it up them, weighed down as it was. Somehow, though, it managed to get us where we needed to go.

The day before we returned home, Jenny wanted to make us all a good meal. We couldn't find an open grocery store anywhere, though. Germany was holding their annual wine festival, and all German businesses were closed for the occasion. The army normally would have had some American px stores open (post exchange shops made available for Army personnel stationed in Germany), but that day they were also closed because it was Columbus Day in the United States. After running out of other options, Jenny remembered that she had the ingredients to make a favorite egg recipe for us.

We later learned that Germany has a policy of leaving eggs unrefrigerated. Apparently, these were purchased at a German grocery store, because that evening everyone in the house got sick with food been to New York City many times and told us she would love to show us around. We agreed and took what turned out to be a delightful trip with her. After touring the city, we took a cruise along the northeast coast to New Brunswick. Charlene's brother and sister-in-law lived in Brooklyn, so she had been in New York City many times, and served as a valuable guide for this trip.

Ann and I had an interesting trip to Northern Canada one year. We took a train to Chicago followed by a ride on the elevated train to Montreal, Quebec, and the surrounding territories. When driving in the area around Quebec we had a real problem with the language barrier. Quebec's residents are quite proud of their French and think that everyone else, even visitors, should speak French as well. We got along fairly well except for the time we tried ordering soft ice cream and were served hard ice cream. This really wasn't a problem, as we enjoy both.

The only other time that we had any troubles with language barriers was when we drove into northern Mexico while on a vacation in San Diego. We had driven through Tijuana, Mexico, and stopped at a shopping center on the south side of town. When it came time to return to San Diego, I had forgotten which way to go. We came across two teenage girls, and I was rather sure they could help us, since most schools teach English. One of the girls knew English but didn't know directions. Fortunately, the other knew directions but didn't know English. Together, they helped get us back to California.

Another notable trip we took was to Amsterdam, Denmark, Norway, and Sweden. The tour was primarily a cruise from Bergen, Norway to the outskirts of Russia and back, but included visits to various locations between. The company that owned the cruise ship was Hurtigruten, which had both freight and passenger lines, so the ship stopped at many ports along the way to deliver fish and other cargo, giving passengers the opportunity to explore the surrounding area. Unfortunately, I got sick on this trip and had a difficult time walking the hills when stopping at the various ports of call. Some people might have enjoyed the chance to simply lounge on the cruise instead of hiking up and down the hills to the various tourist attractions, but I am the kind of man who always likes doing something. Still, the scenery was magnificent, with a number of mountains, which I love, and Ann and I were able to enjoy those even from the ship.

The summer of 1999 was a wonderful time for Ann and me. Annie sang with the Continental Singers, a Christian group of young men and women who were touring the country from west to east that summer. We decided that since we had never been to the western states, we would plan a trip similar to Annie's route so we could see some of her performances as well as a vast portion of our beautiful country. We certainly accomplished that. Our trip lasted 31 days, encompassed 8,000 miles, and took us through sixteen states. Among the many places we visited was the Mall of America in Minnesota. This unbelievable shopping area, the country's largest mall, is really an adventure. It covers 4 million square feet and includes, in addition to its over 500 stores, a theme park with multiple rides, an aquarium, a miniature golf course, and 20,000 parking spaces. Another place we really enjoyed as we headed west was Glacier National Park in Montana. The trip from east to west on the "Going to the Sun" road was gorgeous, but the brochures I had read indicated how beautiful this road was going from west to east. It wasn't that hard for me to decide I wanted to do that, so at the end of the scenic route, we turned around and took the same trip in the opposite direction. I love mountains, so Ann and I were pleased to discover that our second route was beautiful yet different from the first, due to the entirely different mountain views. Another stop we made as we headed toward the state of Washington was a beautiful area in Idaho named Coeur d'Alene, where we picnicked and hiked.

Our next planned stopping point was supposed to be Seattle and a view inside and out of the space needle, but there are very interesting places between Spokane and Seattle, Washington. We stopped along the way to see Grand Coulee Dam as well as a quaint Bavarian village named Leavenworth. After leaving the state of Washington and driving along the Pacific Ocean through Oregon, we headed for the giant redwood trees in northwestern California. We actually drove through several of these massive trees. As our trip continued, we drove around Lake Tahoe. In Salt Lake City, we visited the Mormon Tabernacle, where we attended a service and heard the Mormon Tabernacle Choir; we also viewed the Great Salt Lake. The next day we went to Jackson, Wyoming, a tourist's paradise and the home of Grand Teton National Park. Right outside of the Grand

Tetons is Yellowstone National Park. Yellowstone didn't quite live up to my expectations, but it was still an interesting place where we observed Old Faithful, two great waterfalls, and a number of wild animals. We met up again with Annie in Estes Park, Colorado, and also in Littleton, Colorado. My favorite part of this magnificent trip was seeing Mount Rushmore. I still can't comprehend a project as massive and magnificent as Mount Rushmore. These are just some of the many memories we have from our wonderful vacation in 1999.

In the spring of 1994, I went to a travel agent, curious as to whether I could afford to travel to Alaska with my wife. I had always wanted to go to Alaska, but never thought I could afford to do so. Ann and I liked to plan our own tours, so the agent gave me the costs to fly round-trip to Anchorage and to Fairbanks, the costs of various tours while there, and a sample of typical motel costs. By the time she suggested a cruise, I felt I was already at my limit, but everyone, including the tour director, said a trip to Alaska wouldn't be complete without a cruise. The tour prices on the ship she recommended, Holland America, ranged from $1,400 to $3,700 per person. Cruises are charged by the number of passengers, not by the number of rooms, so we would end up paying between $2,800 and $7,400. I decided that with the airfare and sightseeing, we just couldn't afford this. For two people, even the lowest rate would be over my limit.

As I was leaving the office, another director asked me, "Did I hear you asking about a cruise in Alaska?"

"Yes," I said, "but I don't think I can afford it."

"Did she tell you about the special two-for-one offer for Indiana residents?"

I went back to my agent, who hadn't heard about the special.

"When did you want to take your tour?" she asked. We had promised to babysit for Ken and Deb, who were expecting their third child on July 31, so we told her that and suggested around the middle of August. When she checked into the promotional rates she said, "I've got good news and bad news. The good news is that Holland America does offer a two-for-one rate for Indiana residents, but unfortunately it's only for this July." July 3, 10, 17, and 24 were filled up, but a few spaces were available for July 31.

What could I do, now? At half the price, my dream trip was much more affordable (although we would have to stay in one of the less expensive cabins in the center of the ship). The only problem was that the dates of our trip would likely conflict with the promise we had made to Ken.

When we spoke about it with Ken, though, he was very adamant that we go to Alaska. "We can get others to help," he told us. "We've already had several offers for help with the kids."

Although I felt guilty, I agreed that we should take advantage of this wonderful opportunity. I ordered two $1,800 voyages, for a total $3,600 for both. These would be for a rather small inside cabin, but we realized that most of the time we would not be in our room anyway.

On July 22, I was in the process of planning my agenda when I received a phone call from the Cruise Company that they had overbooked our cruise. They told me that although we had a secure booking, they wanted to give us an incentive to postpone our cruise to August 14. If we would agree to change our plans, they would make the change with the airlines and give us two for the price of one. I reminded them that we already were booked at two-for-one. They were well aware of that, they said, but this new offer was based on our reduced price. In other words, instead of paying $1,800 (originally priced at $3,600), we would get the cruise for $900. This decision was easy since we really preferred the August date anyway. Incidentally, our granddaughter, Olivia Lee, was born on July 31, right on schedule, and we were able to watch Ken and Deb's kids, like we'd originally planned.

On August 10, we were headed to Carmel, Indiana, where my brother, Richard, lives. He was going to take us to the Indianapolis Airport on the following morning. When we arrived there, he informed us that the tour agent had been trying to reach us. We called back only to receive alarming news. The ship had run aground in Ketchikan, Alaska. It was to be taken to Seattle for repairs, and we would have to postpone until September. This seemed rather late in the year to me, considering the weather in Alaska would probably be rather cold, but a trip in September was better than no trip at all.

Although disappointed, Ann and I decided, since our bags were packed and we were already in Carmel, we might as well vacation in Kentucky rather than go back home. We had a good time in Kentucky, but when we arrived back in Auburn, I realized that I needed to call the cruise headquarters to see what they would do about the deposit we had paid.

They were really nice about it and asked if we would be willing to go the following June. I said that would be fine; I had waited fifty-nine years, why not one more? He then said that since we had been so inconvenienced, they would knock off another $600. This made our price $300, with the original price of $3,600 cut in half because of the two-for-one special; the $1,800 cut in half because we agreed to push the trip back to August (the date we had originally wanted to go anyway); and then the additional $600 reduction. In addition, he moved us from a "J" room to an "A" room, a much larger room with a window to the ocean, an outside deck, a hot tub, and a queen-sized bed. On the original brochure, this room would have cost $7,400.

Because of these savings we decided to extend our trip by a week. We also purchased a camcorder so that we can now reminisce by watching our trips on VHS. We used the extra week to see the beautiful Canadian Rockies. We also took a ferry to Vancouver Island, where we saw the Butchart Gardens. Many think that this place has the most magnificent flower gardens in the world. Alaska and the Canadian Rockies are two of my favorite places, and to see both of these at such a savings is just another of the great provisions that God has given me. Truly, this was another *But God* moment.

I have had the privilege of traveling to all fifty states, and many ask me which one I like best. This really is a hard question, but for me it has to be Alaska. Hawaii is beautiful, but since I just love the mountains, I also place Colorado before Hawaii.

Here are a few pictures from our numerous travels over the years:

Dole Plantation in Hawaii

Rose Parade

Albuquerque International Balloon Festival (NM)

One of my favorite spots, Mount Rushmore

A thatched roof house in England

The London Eye
Each car had a bench in the center and glass windows all
around so that a person could see in all directions.

A view in Alaska from our cruise ship (1995)

Canadian Rockies (1995)

Adam and I on Orkney Island (Scotland)

St. Andrews Golf Course in Scotland

Blair Castle in Scotland

Possibly my favorite trip of all was the one we took to Australia and New Zealand in 2005. Even our time spent on the airplane was fascinating. We had traveled to Los Angeles the previous day and enjoyed some of the city prior to our flight on Qantas Airlines. The flight left L.A. at 11:25 p.m. (6:25 p.m. the following day in Melbourne). Qantas is a superb airline, and the plane, a 747-400, was luxurious and huge (75 rows averaging 9 seats across). Each seat had a TV monitor on the back of the seat in the row in front of it. With the headset provided and the armrest control panel, we could choose movies, Nick on Q, selected sporting events, or music of various types. We could see the plane's altitude (38,000 feet), outside temperature (-72 degrees), speed (500 – 560 mph), time in Melbourne (19 hours later than the time in L.A.), hours elapsed, and hours remaining (flight total was 14 hrs. 36 min.); distance elapsed, and distance remaining (total distance 7,960 mi.). The trip was fairly smooth (except for possibly 20 minutes of turbulence), and there was room to move about the cabin and even to do exercises in the rear of the cabin. I did not think the flight seemed nearly as long as we had feared. Our connecting flight to Hobart, Tanzania took only 55 minutes.

It was Monday evening when we arrived, because when we crossed the International Date Line we lost a day. Tasmania is an island on the south side of Australia. The airport at Hobart was quite small. After collecting our baggage we were picked up by our tour bus and taken to our first hotel. Hobart is the Capital of Tasmania, which is one of the six states in Australia (but on a separate island). Hobart is nearly the southernmost state of Australia, but is cooler than the rest of the continent, since the North is the closest to the equator. The local temperature was 22 degrees Celsius; 72 degrees Fahrenheit. Incidentally, conversion from Celsius to Fahrenheit is easy if one knows the formula: Celsius times 9 divided by 5 plus 32. In the evening we gathered together to meet our Tour Guide, Barry. This turned out to be rather humbling and embarrassing. We had gone to our room to relax, but were apparently more tired than we had known. The room telephone woke us up. Barry, our tour director, had called wondering where we were. I am sure that the entire group supposed we would be tardy the entire trip, but actually there would be no further problems in the entire remaining schedule, even from us.

On Tuesday, January 25, I toured several spots on our trip with our driver, Arthur. Unfortunately Ann had become sick during the night and was unable to go on the tour of Tasmania. Arthur lived in the area and gave us many interesting facts about Tasmania as we rode along. The landscape in Tasmania wasn't much to look at as it is very dry on this eastern part of the lower island (about 20 in. of rain per year), but many of the lake and river views were outstanding. The water was the bluest blue I have ever seen; and the air was amazingly pure (as a matter of fact, Tasmania air quality is used as a 100% standard when grading air purity in other places in the world).

We stopped at the Tasmanian Devil Sanctuary where we witnessed the feeding of Tasmanian Devils (a carnivorous animal with jaws 9 times more powerful than a pit bull). They eat their entire prey: the outer skin, the gizzards, and even the bones. This place had lots of kangaroos and cockatoos. We were able to walk about them freely. Incidentally, I figured out the difference between a wallaby and a Joey. It is somewhat like the difference between a pony and a colt in that they are similar in size, but a completely different animal. After leaving there, we went to Port Arthur Historic Site (previously a prison and now said to be Tanzania's premier tourist attraction). Arthur, our driver, discussed a number of things about this site, and then we were able to roam about as we pleased. It has not been used as a prison for many years, and reminded me somewhat of San Francisco's Alcatraz in that it was a former prison now closed and that it was difficult to escape from. In the 1800's it was a penal colony for convicts. On the way back to Hobart we toured several spectacular rock formations: Tasman Arch, Devil's Kitchen, and the Blow Hole. We arrived back at dinnertime.

One of the real advantages of a tour group is the service provided by others. On this trip the tour guide, the Hotel Bellmen, and the bus driver take care of everything. They pick the bags up from beside our door, load them on the bus, remove them when we arrive at the next hotel, and even take them to the check-in at the airports if we are to make another flight. They get our boarding passes and even take the bags off the carousel at the airport. We are only responsible for our carry-on bags and ourselves. The day in Melbourne was on our own (Barry and our driver gave us a number of suggestions for things to see and do). It was a national holiday in Australia (Australian Day – January 26, in honor of Captain Cook, who discovered Australia). Melbourne had outstanding fireworks in the evening. We also took the city tram downtown to the botanical gardens, to Fitzroy Gardens, and to view Melbourne, a beautiful and a planned city.

On Thursday, January 27, we were on our own until 3:30 in the afternoon. Then we went to Phillip Island, a 3-hour bus ride. The little penguins (formerly known as fairy penguins because of their small size) make their home on Phillip Island and are the largest colony of fairy penguins in the world. At sunset these penguins come ashore in bunches. They waddle ashore in parade fashion, crossing the beach to feed their young under the bleachers where we are sitting to watch. Unfortunately, we could not take pictures. Photography is prohibited because the flashes will hurt their eyes. By the time we returned to our rooms, it was midnight.

Our night was a short one, and Friday, the 28th, would be a superb but busy one. We departed at 7:30 a.m. for the airport for our trip to Ayres Rock in the outback. This flight was 2 hours and 10 minutes, and we entered into a unique time zone where we would change our watches by ½ hour from 11 a.m. to 10:30. When we stepped off our plane (which was outside the terminal at this small airport), we could really feel how hot it was. It was 113 degrees Fahrenheit. We were now in the outback, Central Australia, in an area where the Aborigines live. It is the only area that is home to approximately 500,000 dromedary (one-hump) camels. The two outstanding attractions here were absolutely awesome, but so was the heat, very uncomfortable. Ayres Rock, which is known as Uluru to the Aboriginal people and considered by them to be sacred ground, is located in Kata Tjuta National Park. It is the largest rock on earth (covering 1,200 acres and measuring 2.1 miles long, 1.5 miles wide, and 1,100 feet high (taller than the Empire State Building). It has a red sandstone cover. About 20 miles away (you can see it from Uluru) are the Olgas – a series of 36 huge rocks that reach a height of 1,790 feet. Both sights were too huge for a still picture. On Friday evening we returned to the rock to see how the setting sun could create many changing colors on the rock. Unfortunately, a rare thunderstorm developed and we could not see the sunset, nor could we see the changing colors. I did observe unusual lightning bolts and a sandstorm, however.

On Saturday, January 29, we flew to Alice Springs, one of the few Australian cities not along a coast. That evening was very probably the highlight of this trip. We went into the outback, even taking a dirt road back at least five miles. Rod Steinert and his family cooked the dinner (chicken and steak). This man was really funny. He made us a dessert, which he called "Spotted Dog." It was a very humorous presentation. He took huge handfuls of flour and put them into a heavy-duty kettle (the kind used for an open fire). Then he went to a huge bowl and mixed up the dough using his large hands to mix the ingredients. He used two half quarts of currants (making note of the importance of using 2 half quarts and never to use 1 full quart which would never work). He added sugar, baking powder, and milk. He just threw in each ingredient by memory, never using measuring instruments of any kind, while all the time explaining how important it was to use accurate measurements. Stirring well, he poured this in on top of the flour into the kettle. Then he put a heavy lid on it and put it on the hot coals to bake while we ate our dinner.

The dinner was delightful. First they gave us a cup of soup, and then we got the rest of our dinner from the line. We had chicken and steak and vegetables, all of which was prepared by Rod's wife and daughters. While eating, another person played the guitar and sang. We even had a time to sing along. After this we ate the "Spotted Dog," which was very good. Rod pointed out for us The Southern Cross plus various other stars, which really showed up marvelously in the purified clear air. Hardly anyone lives in the central part of Australia, and there is not the pollution that we have in the states.

On Sunday morning, January 30, we went to an Aboriginal Village, very near to where we had eaten our meal the previous evening. Rod, the same person who had served us the previous evening, explained about these tribes and their customs. There are 300-350 Aboriginal Tribes, all speaking different languages (some 3,000 dialects) and having different customs. The tribe we visited was the Wolferee Tribe from northwest of Alice Springs. This tribe has a population of 1,600. The same geographical area of England would have a population of 68,000,000. They live in groups of 18-20 people.

Rod explained that one of the reasons there are so few of the Aboriginal people is that, because of their environment, menopause begins at about age 24. He estimated that there are 400,000 in the country with a life span averaging 45 years. They believe that before the white man there were only kangaroos and emus, no domesticated animals and no agriculture. The Aboriginals have very bad hygiene. They needed all of their water for drinking, so washing was not important to them. Just 80-90 years ago, people in this area of Central Australia were living in the Stone Age. Many times, they live in the dry bed of the river, not so much because they cannot afford more, but because they are comfortable with it. They just have different customs from us. For example, they care little about possessions. For them, having little is better because they do not have as much to care for. Houses and things have little value. They do not care how they look or how much they have, as long as they survive. Marriage is arranged; however, this is changing.

The Aborigines should not be judged based on our culture, because they have a different culture. Most of them go to school. They rub body fats on themselves to keep warm (although I do not think it hardly ever gets cold here even in their winter). Their beliefs (called Dreamland) are that nothing existed in the beginning except for spiritual life above the ground. They believe that mountains, streams, etc. were created by spiritual beings (I guess that they do not believe in evolution either). They do not have a written word. Their language has been passed down from generation to generation by singing, in nursery rhyme fashion. In this way of singing it is believed that their history has been maintained fairly accurately and not continually changed. Aboriginal paintings are their way of telling stories about their culture. They do not talk about the dead because they believe that the dead still have spirits. This is also the reason that they do not want their pictures taken. They do not want their spirits to spread. They name their spirits, usually based on the animals of the region.

After leaving here we went to the airport for our 2-hour flight to Darwin on the Northern tip of Australia. There we boarded another bus and went to Kakadu National Park. Our hotel (Gagudju Crocodile Holiday Inn) was located in the park and was shaped like a crocodile. Along the way we saw termite mounds at least 6 feet tall. The termites are so thick in this area of Australia that they need to use a special treatment on the wood for houses, and they have metal telephone poles instead of wooden ones.

On Monday morning, we took a walking tour to see more aboriginal drawings. These were on another large rock formation in the park. Then we took a 1¾-hour cruise on the Yellow River. Because it was in the wet season, we were also able to cruise a billabong (body of water). We saw a crocodile and a large number of various birds, and while on the South Alligator River we saw thousands of fruit bats.

Tuesday, February 1, was a travel day, well timed since it has been so hot and humid, our glasses getting steamed up just walking out of our hotel rooms. It was humid and close to 100 degrees throughout the Northern Territory. First we drove from Kakadu National Park back to Darwin, about 150 miles. We stopped at a couple of roadside parks along the way. Our guide, Barry, was very good about this. We never went more than 2 hours without a bathroom stop. This day was hard, however, because we were on the bus or in a plane nearly all day. Our flight was from Darwin to Brisbane and Brisbane to Cairns (if you look at a map, this is like Minneapolis to Atlanta to Boston). We arrived at our hotel at 10:30 p.m. ready for bed. Our hotel, Pacific International Cairns, was in another great location, right across the street from the Great Barrier Reef. It was a welcome relief to leave the flies. They were so much of a bother in Central Australia that we actually bought a net to place over our heads to keep our sanity. They are no problem, however, along the coastal regions.

On Wednesday we never got on a bus or a plane. After a great breakfast we walked across the street to the pier and got on a boat to take us to Green Island, a 45-minute trip on a rather fast boat. It was a beautiful summer day (possibly a little too hot and humid). From the island we took a glass-bottomed boat where we encountered many large and beautiful fish. We also, while on the island, visited a crocodile pavilion, where we watched them feed the crocodile. We also watched them feeding turtles and saw some beautiful fish. The beach was lovely, and the water was some of the clearest I had ever seen, a requirement for a barrier reef.

On Thursday, February 3, we were able to sleep in, eat a late breakfast, and even do some shopping. We boarded a bus for the airport at 10:45 a.m. Cairns is a tourist city as could be easily detected by all of the hotels and motels we saw along the way. Our watches changed again today. We moved them ahead one hour as we approached Sydney, and arrived at about 4:30 p.m. (12:30 in the morning in our Eastern Time Zone back in the states). The scenery as we were flying into Sydney was possibly the most delightful I had ever seen.

Friday, February 4, was another marvelous day. First we went to Koala Park, where we had our picture taken with a koala. The lady was holding one that we could pet, and there were seven or so in the eucalyptus trees. Their diet consists of nothing other than eucalyptus leaves, and that is what they were eating as we watched. Surprisingly, they do not drink water. We also were able to see kangaroos and wallabies, dingoes and wombats, and a number of beautiful birds while at the park (Now I know what you get when you cross a dingo with a wombat; you get a dingbat!). Next we had our group picture taken at a spectacular scenic spot, the backdrop being the Sydney Harbor and the Sydney Opera House. To think that we had always seen so many pictures of this place and now we were seeing it in person. We took a tour of the city, but the traffic was so heavy that it reminded me of Los Angeles. Twenty million people live in Australia, and five million of them live in Sydney. When you add in the population of Melbourne and Perth (a West Coast city that we did not visit), you realize that there is little population in the rest of Australia. Our hotel, Crowne Plaza Darling Harbor, was close to Darling Harbor, a lovely part of Sydney. Our dinner tonight (included in our package) was at the Summit Restaurant, which revolves while you are eating. We were 541 feet above the city (if my conversion from 165 meters is correct). Since our dinnertime was more than one full revolution, we were able to see a lot of beautiful sights, because Sydney is truly a beautiful city. We saw the Sydney Opera House, Sydney Harbor Bridge (the largest one-span bridge in the world), and Olympic Park, where the 2000 Olympics were held.

On Saturday morning we took a boat tour on Sydney Harbor (Captain Cook Boats). It was really a nice cruise and took a little over an hour. The sights, especially the fabulous estates lining the harbor banks, were so much easier to see from the harbor than from the streets. At 4:15 we left for the Sydney Opera House. This was the night that all of us had brought dress clothes for, and everyone looked so great. We first got a tour of the Concert Hall and the Opera Theatre and learned a number of facts about this building, which were fascinating to me, probably because I'm an accountant. The building occupies 5.5 hectares (13.6 sq. mi.). It was estimated to cost seven million dollars and ended up costing one hundred and two million Australian Dollars (nearly 15 times the original estimate). It was begun in 1956, and because of Governmental red tape, the unique design, and a change in architects, it was not completed until 1973 (17 years later).

Sunday, February 6, was a travel day. We left Australia and headed east to Christchurch, New Zealand, (a distance of 1,369 miles). The remainder of our trip would be by bus. We were told that the population of New Zealand is 3.88 million (in people that is. They also have 40,000,000 sheep; 6,000,000 dairy cows; and 2,500,000 deer). There are no snakes and no predators. As far as we could tell, there are also no mosquitoes or flies, and the people can leave their windows and doors open. I had thought that flying into Sydney was beautiful, and it was because of the harbors and waterways and buildings. Flying into Christchurch was also spectacular because of the mountain ranges.

Monday was to be one of the highlights of our trip as the scenery was to be spectacular. Unfortunately, for only the second time on this vacation, we had rain. This time, we also had a low fog and low clouds. The views were still nice, but could have been so much better with sunshine. I got the idea that this particular portion of the world, in Milford Sound, has these conditions most of the time. We did see many waterfalls, however, and we would only have seen the two natural waterfalls (Bowen Falls and Sterling Falls) if it had not rained. The other falls dry up when it stops raining. We saw fjords, which they say were carved out by glaciers. A "sound" is carved out by water. We could tell by the multitude of buses at Milford Sound and at many places along the way that this area was indeed a huge tourist attraction. Many of the tour groups were foreign, a majority being of Asian nationality – Japanese, Chinese, and Vietnamese. As we were heading back to Queenstown, the weather cleared, and the views, especially around Lake Wakatipu, were magnificent.

Certainly Tuesday, February 8, had to be another of the highlights of this trip. We elected to go on an optional *The Lord of the Rings* tour. Although we had not seen the movie, we had heard that our daughter, daughter-in-law, and some of our grandchildren had seen it. Also we had heard that the area had been selected for the movie because of the spectacular sights. Choosing this location was a wise decision for the moviemakers, and choosing this side tour proved to be a wise decision for

Ann and I. We had taken a chance on the weather, which turned out to be perfect. We got to the sights by an open jeep, the only means of getting into some of the areas (other than possibly helicopter). Our guide, Allison, drove us through various streams and up huge embankments. It was lots of fun, and the views were spectacular.

Allison did a great job of explaining at each of our stops, many high in the various mountain areas in nearby Queensland, which scenes from the movie took place in the particular area. Each of the jeeps had a name taken from one of the characters in the movie. We were on the jeep named "Pippin." The entire series of movies (three in all), each being three hours in length, were all filmed in sequence and entirely in New Zealand, primarily in the areas we visited. We viewed the Kawarau River and saw many views of the mountain area named "The Remarkables" for obvious reasons. They are not terribly tall (approximately 6,900 feet tall), but are remarkably beautiful. We saw fences way up on top when we got there, and in answer to my question, Allison told us that Merino sheep graze there. They move them down in the winter to below the snow line and then return them come spring.

We stopped just outside Arrowtown where some panned for gold. Arrowtown is a gold-mining town that has been maintained to look as it did in 1860, when the town was busy with people searching for gold. In the evening we took the gondolas to the top of one of the mountains where we were served dinner at The Skyline Restaurant, another huge buffet dinner.

On Wednesday, February 9, we headed to Mount Cook National Park, making stops at Arrowtown and Omarama. Just outside Queenstown we saw someone bungee jumping from a tall bridge. We were informed that bungee jumping had originated at this very sight. After this, we noticed that it is quite popular in New Zealand. The views along the way to Mount Cook were beautiful, especially during the final 50 or so miles before arriving at Mount Cook (New Zealand's highest mountain at 12,313 feet, and the only one we saw with snow in the summer). The view from our hotel was magnificent. We arrived at 3:15 p.m., which allowed us time to walk the trails or just look at the mountains before our 6:45 dinner.

On Thursday, we drove to Christchurch, the largest city on the South Island. Our stay while at Christchurch was right downtown. It was named Rydges Christchurch. As we continued throughout our bus trips, Barry and the driver continued to give us knowledge of the area and the country. For example, today we learned that the South Island of New Zealand has many earthquakes (because it is on a fault line). Getting around is so much easier even though they have no interstate highways, primarily because of the reduced population. There are approximately 1½ million people on the South Island and 3½ million on the North Island (and in total about 45 million sheep).

On Friday, February 11, we boarded the Trans-Alpine Express in Christchurch, which took us for a scenic ride through the Southern Alps of New Zealand. We rode the train east as far as Arthur's Pass (approximately 75 miles). This was only the third day with clouds and rain, but the scenery was still very good, with mountains and lakes all along the way. By this time, however, we are getting spoiled by all of the beautiful mountain scenes, so it was not nearly as spectacular as in the Queenstown area. The whole area is mountainous, and our train went through 16 tunnels along the way. We returned to Christchurch by bus.

On Saturday, we were driven from Christchurch to Picton. In Picton we left our bus and boarded a ferryboat for our trip from the south island to the north island to Wellington, the Capital of New Zealand. The drive to Picton was very pleasant, following the Pacific Ocean along New Zealand's east coast. We even saw seals on the rocks as we were going along the coast. Both the bus ride and the cruise continued to show off many of the wonderful mountain ranges throughout New Zealand.

On our Sunday morning tour, we learned additional information about Wellington and New Zealand in general. For example, there are an average of three earthquakes per day in New Zealand (although some are not even felt), and sometimes there are as many as six or seven. Our city tour took us to the top of Mount Victoria. Many deluxe homes are built on various levels of the mountain, and they are very picturesque. The homes are much higher than the garage area, and they have cable cars to carry their groceries and goods from the car to their houses. The view from the top of Mount Victoria was lovely in every direction. On two sides we could see the Cook Strait (where we had ferried in on Saturday), and on the other two sides we could see the residential district and the city. On our city tour, we saw the government buildings (Wellington being the capital of New

Zealand) and the Botanical Gardens, which had one of the finest display of flowers I have seen anywhere.

Monday, February 14, Valentines Day, was primarily a travel day. There were still many mountain scenes along the way, and we stopped at Huka Falls, a delightful break. The falls were not high, but there were fast rushing rapids here. We had chosen to stay with a New Zealand family that evening instead of at a hotel. We are so glad we made this decision, because we really enjoyed our time at Inala Nalood. This is the name that Les and Christine Doolan (the couple we stayed with) called their place (*inala* means a peaceful place, and Nalood is Doolan spelled backwards). Christine works for an attorney (as a secretary), but somehow still has time to keep immaculate grounds. They have acres of flowers and vegetables and lovely rolling hills. They also have two donkeys. Christine, in addition, has astronomy as a hobby, and she took the time to point out several stars that cannot be seen from our part of the world, including The Southern Cross, The Diamond Cross, and The False Cross. She also pointed out that the moon, which was in the first quarter, was backwards from the way we see it from our portion of the earth because it curves in the opposite direction, a fact that I found to be extremely interesting.

We had a full morning on Tuesday. First we went to the Whakarewarewa Thermal Reserve. The reserve is keeping the Maori Tribe's customs alive by teaching Maori skills of carving and weaving. We witnessed this and also witnessed some of the bubbling and steaming terraces of Rotorua, an area somewhat like Yellowstone where the underground volcanic activity creates geysers. We also went to the Agrodome, a place we found to be very interesting and entertaining. We saw about fifteen different type of sheep, witnessed sheep shearing, and also saw a sheep dog herd a group of sheep into a pen. Since we had seen literally thousands of sheep throughout our tour of New Zealand, we felt this was very appropriate. We also went to Rainbow Springs, where we visited trout and birds. Here we saw a kiwi, the symbol for New Zealand. It is a flightless bird, one that they fear will become extinct. Rainbow Springs is attempting to rescue the kiwi from extinction. We were not allowed to photograph the bird. They are a nocturnal animal and are in an environment, which is kept dark. I believe it is the only time we have ever seen a kiwi.

Wednesday, February 16, was the final day of a wonderful adventure. Our primary goal this day was to get to the Auckland Airport to return to Los Angeles. Some, a group of 19, would continue on to Fiji, and one couple, John and Kathy, would stay in Auckland two days and then fly to Fiji before returning to the States. On the way to Auckland, however, we had time to stop at Waitomo Caves, one of the North Island's main attractions. The caves are lit by thousands of glowworms. We found that the glowworm is really a larva, a stage in the development of a gnat. The spokesperson told us that thousands of people come every year to see the glowworms, and that not nearly as many would come if they advertised them as larvae. Therefore, they came up with the term "glowworm," which could be where the Mills Brothers' song title came from. The glowworm emits a bright light to attract food and builds a nest of mucus and silk in the shape of a hollow tube, which is attached to the cave roof by a series of fine silk like threads. After seeing the "worms" glow inside the cave, I felt that "glowworm" was an accurate term. While on the way to Auckland we also passed areas where kiwi fruit grow (I had never associated kiwi fruit with New Zealand). We also had time to ascend Mount Eden in the city of Auckland before getting to the airport. It was another fascinating view, as is all of the mountain scenery in New Zealand. What an awe-inspiring country it is.

We flew out at around 9:10 p.m. in the evening after spending another day in New Zealand, and then were able to spend the day once again in Los Angeles, since we arrived shortly after noon on this same day. We had regained the day that we had lost at the beginning of the trip by re-crossing the International Date Line.

I have been greatly blessed in all areas of my life, which I have been abundantly reminded of as I enumerate some of my favorite adventures. Ann and I have been able to travel to every one of our fifty states and to fourteen countries. Certainly the nature of my occupation accounted for much of this; although I worked many hours a large portion of each year, being self-employed and being able to adjust my hours the rest of the year gave me tremendous flexibility to plan trips.

While traveling, I have employed two customs that really worked for Ann and me. One is that for the most part, I planned our trips completely. This allowed us to visit only the places we wanted and to determine the amount of time we wished to stay at each location. It also helped us immensely in budgeting our trips. The other thing I made a point of was taking detailed notes on every trip. These notes have been invaluable to me as I reminisce about God's blessings in my life, and are the reason I made such a long and detailed story about our trip to Australia and New Zealand.

13

But God

● ● ● ● ● ● ● ● ● ●

IT IS RATHER AMAZING TO me that God loves us so very much even when we are ignoring Him completely. Many of the *But God* moments in my life took place before I really knew Him. Now as I write my memoirs, I truly realize that God knew and loved me long before I knew and loved Him.

Those who enjoy my testimony the most are those who knew me before I knew Jesus. Of all the things that God does, the most fabulous thing is seeing how He can change a man's heart. I was really never a bad person. In a way, I suppose that is what made coming to Jesus so difficult. All of my life, I knew about Jesus, which made me believe I was a good Christian. My parents taught me the Ten Commandments and insisted I be in church and Sunday school every Sunday morning. I felt two hours of church every week was plenty for me. For a while, I went with a girl from Kendallville whose idea of a good time was going to church, and that seemed rather dumb to me. I think maybe I complied on one of our dates, but when she continued to prefer church to other activities, I felt it necessary to break up with her.

When I met Ann, I had no idea she was Catholic until I fell in love with her, by which point I couldn't care less. Ann was just as set in her Catholic lifestyle as I was in my Lutheran one. The more we dated, however, the more we fell in love. Both of my parents and her mother tried to discourage us, and I suppose that the harder they tried, the more we wanted to get married. She would not agree to leave the Catholic Church, but I had heard too many teachings against the Catholic Church to go to her church.

It is rather astonishing to me as I look back on where each of us were in our individual Christian lives. She was a girl who had been taught that Catholic teachings were the only correct teachings. I had been taught the same thing about Lutheran teachings. Furthermore, my church had a philosophy in the 1940s and 50s that Catholics had everything wrong in their teachings and even went so far as to emphasize that we should have nothing to do with them. Whether this emphasis was in all Lutheran churches or just the one I attended, I do not know, but I did know I was in a dilemma. I really liked Ann, and I wasn't willing to give her up. I loved my parents, though, and I could see that I was disappointing them.

Being devoted to the Lutheran Church and being devoted to God, however, are vastly different things. I didn't pray about my relationship with Ann. I didn't study the Bible to see what God's Word said. Being so weak in faith made it so much easier for each of us to justify how we could make our marriage work. We figured that we would be together six days each week plus twenty-two hours on Sunday. Surely we could go our separate ways for two hours each week. Our spiritual lives were certainly not that important. We came to the agreement that our marriage would be a success because we would leave God out of it. We agreed to never discuss religion. We also agreed that we would never ask each other to attend church with us.

Even writing about this makes me shudder to think where we were at that time. *But God* desired something entirely different. Leaving God out of the picture had to be the worst possible way to start a marriage. Thankfully, though, we now realize that to make a marriage succeed, a couple needs to put God at the very center of their marriage. Instead of going our separate ways on Sunday, Ann and I should have formed a common bond with Jesus, praying and reading the Word with each other regularly.

At the time, though, I thought our marriage was successful. By 1972, we had four great children (Carol hadn't been born yet). I had advanced quickly in my profession and was a partner in a rather large and successful accounting firm by age thirty-six. Ann knew, though, that all was not well. We joined Club Olympia and started doing the things "successful" people do, but frankly, we weren't having much fun. She felt that our life was empty, lacking something to give it true purpose and meaning.

I was awakened to this in 1980, when Ann told me that she had decided to leave me. She wasn't sure where she would go, but she had taken all that she could take in living with a workaholic who rarely spent time in conversation with her or took time to truly invest in our relationship. To say I was shocked would be an understatement. Apparently, we had a lack of communication, because I had no idea that Ann was unhappy. At this time in my life, my idea was that Ann had a truly happy life since I had a good income and was content in my job and social status. I guess I had been too blind to see what marriage really should be.

But God had other plans for us. When Ann saw how distressed I was at the idea of her leaving, she agreed go to Christian marriage counseling with me. Through this experience, I began to realize something that no one had ever explained to me before: the way to a woman's heart is not through material possessions. I had provided for Ann's physical needs, but never given her my time or conversation. I loved and admired my wife but had never learned how to show it. Ann and I prayed, and all who heard of our problem prayed. God saw my heart, Ann saw my grief, and God allowed me to make the many changes required to make a marriage work. I am so blessed that Ann gave me another chance.

One thing stands out as I sum up my wonderful life. Because of a mistake that I made which almost cost me my marriage, I learned an important lesson: "Our wives are not as interested in our money as they are in our quality time. If they love us, they can't get enough of the precious time we take to spend with them." Now Ann and I read the Word and pray with each other every morning. What I had considered the most terrible thing that could ever happen turned out to be about the best thing I could ever imagine. What Satan intended for evil, God intended for good. These changes, however, did not occur, nor could they have, before each of us had personal relationships with Jesus.

In 1972, Ann was helping Sister Beatrice in one of the classes at St. Vincent Catholic School where our children attended school at the time. Sister Beatrice, knowing Ann liked to read, gave her the book "Catholic Pentecostals" to read. When Ann later expressed how much she had enjoyed the book, Sister Beatrice told her about a group of Pentecostals who were meeting at the Crosier House on Friday nights. The very part of the book that would have turned me off fascinated her. It was about something called "speaking in tongues." Ann told me that she would like to attend one of these meetings. I had never interfered with her churchgoing, but I certainly didn't want to join her. Two hours each week at church was plenty for me, but I told her that if she wished to go, it was fine with me. I loved to listen to the Detroit Tigers' baseball games, and I was content to stay home and do so while she met with the Pentecostal group. The meeting started at 7:30, so I expected her back by 9:00 at the latest. At 10:00, I became quite concerned, and at 11:15, I decided to call the Crosier House. They told me that the meeting had just ended, they were having fellowship, and my wife would be home shortly. I didn't even know what fellowship was, but I surely felt sorry for her. I got fidgety if Sunday's service exceeded one hour. I couldn't even imagine a church meeting lasting 3½ hours. I could really imagine how upset Ann would be. To my surprise, though, just the opposite happened. From the moment my wife walked through the door, I could see that she was so excited and had really enjoyed the meeting.

She really enjoyed the meetings and began attending as many as she could. She also developed new habits, and although some of them seemed ridiculous to me, I could see that Ann was swiftly becoming a different person. She was a happy person who no longer became as angry when things went wrong. 2 Corinthians 5:17 really fit: "Therefore, if anyone is in Christ, he is a new creation; the old has gone, the new has come!" It took awhile, but I gradually grew to want the change I saw in her. After several weeks of seeing her beam after attending the Friday night meetings, I became curious. I figured that maybe I should go with her. I didn't really want to, but as her husband, I believed it was my responsibility to protect her from false teachings and make sure she wasn't getting into anything too radical.

So one Friday night, I attended my first Pentecostal meeting with Ann. The whole thing seemed rather strange to me. First of all, no one sat in pews. Instead, they sat around in a circle singing praise songs with their hands raised, led by someone playing guitar. Afterwards, I told Ann that this in itself was undoctrinal, since the only way to worship Jesus was with an organ, or possibly a piano. These people greeted each other with hugs, men even hugging other men. All everyone wanted to talk about was Jesus. It seemed strange that the men didn't even talk about baseball or other sports. After that first meeting, I sure didn't want to go back. As I kept thinking about what I had seen and observed (now I would say it was the Holy Spirit at work), it sparked another series of thoughts in my mind. These people had an intangible aura about them that intrigued me, and I wanted to figure out what it was.

But after attending a second time I became confused. I was beginning to enjoy these meetings; at the same time, however, I also started to wonder if these teachings were contrary to Lutheran beliefs. I wasn't so concerned about whether or not they were biblical; rather, I was concerned about whether or not they contradicted the Lutheran doctrine. So at about 12:30 in the morning I got up, put some clothes on, and went down the street a couple of blocks to where my pastor, Pastor Hoerger lived. This seemed awkward, but definitely necessary since I had to find out if we were getting into a cult or something.

Pastor was gracious, and after he got dressed, we walked around the block several times, then sat down across from my house and talked for some time. When he realized how serious I was and knew how much I needed Christ in my life, he suggested that he and his wife go with us to the following Friday night meeting. He likely wanted to encourage me more than he wanted to experience the meeting. This was really another of the turning points in my relationship with Christ, because if Pastor Hoerger had told me not to become involved with this group, I surely would have listened.

One Sunday Ann's group had a picnic in Huntington. I agreed to go with her because I love picnics and games. These people sure knew how to make people happy. They were having lots of games, and everyone was so nice to one another and having a good time. I was really starting to fit in and enjoy myself when all of a sudden, right in the middle of a horseshoe game, they made an announcement that everyone was going to meet for a prayer meeting. I was shocked and really upset, but I sat in on it. After all, what else could I do? It ruined the whole day for me, though. I had clearly come to the point where I enjoyed the people and the worship, but I certainly didn't have the personal relationship with God that made time with Him better than playing games.

In 1975, a Full Gospel Regional Meeting was being held in Troy, Michigan. Troy is a suburb of Detroit, and I was a Detroit Tiger fan. Ann suggested that we go. Although I didn't really want to go to the convention, I wanted to please Ann. If the Tigers were in town, I thought, I could go to the afternoon session and then take the boys to the game in the evening. I checked the schedule and found out a game was scheduled for the night of the meeting. However, after prepaying the Convention fees and securing the hotel where the convention was being held, I discovered that I had checked a prior year's schedule, and that the Tigers were scheduled to play on the West Coast during the time we were in Detroit. I rather enjoyed myself at the meeting despite this, but God and His delightful sense of humor used my love of baseball to get me to attend.

It was through these Pentecostal meetings that I found out about "Full Gospel Business Men," a Christian Charismatic group started by Demos Shakarian. After I began attending these meetings, I had mixed feelings. I enjoyed the testimonies, but speaking in tongues and being slain in the Spirit were new to me and still made me uncomfortable. Others could see this, and I know that many people were praying for me in this period of my life. One of these people was "Mac" McDougall. He invited me to a Full Gospel meeting in Angola. I found out that the featured speaker was Norbert Selking, a man from Ann's hometown of Decatur. I also found out that he was a Lutheran. I jumped at the chance to hear him speak. If he was Lutheran, then surely he could set all of these crazy people straight. I was wrong again. He went along with all of the things that every other member of Full Gospel did, but like Ann, he appeared to have it all together. I didn't have the nerve to go forward at the altar call, but I did go to him after the meeting to discuss some of my concerns. After answering many questions, he prayed with me, and I received the baptism of the Holy Spirit.

Though Ann had been changing rapidly since she first started attending these meetings, I finally started to notice the difference in her. She was reading the Bible regularly. Although she had never been a worldly girl, she really began to change. She quit partaking of the mixed drinks that we occasionally made, she had a more beautiful disposition, and she began saying "Praise the Lord" for everything, even when something bad happened. When we wanted to go on a picnic but it started to rain, she would say "Praise God," which sort of stumped me. I didn't even praise God when we had sunshine. Why we should praise Him for rain was beyond me. I began to recognize His hand when things went my way, but I was still a long way from praising Him in everything.

A sample of what kind of person my wife has become through the years of her relationship with God can be seen in a character sketch Annie wrote for a high school project shortly before she graduated:

> She sits on her bed, prayer cards in hand. Who would ever imagine that this woman was changing the world in this moment? Yet as I watch her lips move in silent prayer, I know that lives are being transformed because of this simple act.
>
> I grew up watching my Grandmother pray. Each evening she would retire to her bedroom, pull out a manila envelope filled with cards and paper after paper covered with prayers, both short term and long term requests. Her family, friends, church leaders, and Government officials all had a place of honor when their names were written on those cards.
>
> She continues this practice to this day. At times, I lie on her bed just enjoying her company and watching her pray. Her closed eyes, as she quietly prays, reveal that she knows well the contents of each card. Furthermore, the fact that she has many prayers memorized from repetition demonstrates her determination and commitment in her daily petitions to God.
>
> She finishes one card and looks up to give me a warm smile as she shuffles the papers in her hand. I grin back and silently thank God for the wonderful relationship He has given me with my Grandmother. She has such a love for me—for everyone for that matter. I reach for her soft hand, and she gladly squeezes mine as she continues to pray. I remember how these same hands use to mete out discipline, but they also continued to comfort me each

time I came to her in tears. They still give a warm hug or hold my hands in prayer when I am hurting. Those hands are a reflection of her heart as she serves her family, calms an irate husband, holds her newest Grandchild, and does so much more.

As my eyes move to her face, I notice the lines that crease her face. My Grandma was not always the woman she is now. There was a time in which she did not know God. I have heard the stories of anger, bitterness, and fear. The wrinkles around her eyes are a reminder of those days past. In her eyes now is a joy and determination that is evidence of the fact that she loves serving the Lord. I sigh and again thank God for the woman He made my Grandmother to be. Just happy to be with her, I curl up next to her. She puts her arm around me and holds the cards in the other hand. It does not matter to her that I am now seventeen. I will always be her special little girl. She will always be my devoted Grandma. I know she will be praying and continuing to make a difference in the lives of people around her as long as she is able; and I know that I am one of those people. As I fall asleep listening to her voice, I know that God is listening to her heart; and I know He is pleased.

I wasn't the only one affected by the changes in my wife. Our family and friends have all greatly benefited from her transformation in Christ.

During this time in our lives, I learned an important truth. When either a wife or husband begins to receive God's joy, they obviously want the same thing for their spouse. Many will begin to beg and coax, sometimes even complaining that their mate hasn't caught up with them. Thank God, Ann never made that mistake. She would invite, but never beg. She never nagged me or told me how lost I was. I thank God for that, because if she had, I probably would still be lost today. It wouldn't have worked anyway, because I thought I was already saved. After all, I was an usher in my church, and had even been president of the congregation one year. Ann just kept getting more and more radiant, and her changes were more obvious than ever to me. I later noticed that Peter had written about her in 1 Peter 3:

> *Wives, in the same way, be submissive to your husbands so that, if any of them do not believe the word, they may be won over without talk by the behavior of their wives, when they see the purity and reverence of your lives. Your beauty should not come from outward adornment, such as braided hair and the wearing of gold jewelry or fine clothes. Instead it should be that of your inner self, the unfading beauty of a gentle and quiet spirit, which is of great worth in God's sight.*

As I grew in my relationship with Christ, I saw more and more the inward beauty of my wife.

I was beginning to enjoy those monthly meetings of Full Gospel Businessmen, but fought every new aspect along the way. Being slain in the Spirit was a new experience, and although I respected many of the individuals I had seen falling over in the Spirit, I hesitated. I, a college graduate, was far too intelligent and sophisticated to have this happen to me. Although Ann saw this and speaking in tongues as spiritual events, I fought against them. Until it happened to me, I thought everyone was acting. I have since been slain in the Spirit and spoken in tongues, and therefore stopped doubting them as much; some people abuse these gifts, though, and sometimes I still question whether it's God's Holy Spirit or an acting job.

At this point, I was a regular attendee at Full Gospel Meetings, and even started attending regional and state meetings. The first of these was rather eventful. The meeting was held at Lake Wawasee, and I paid the registration fee, expecting to attend on Thursday through Saturday. However, on Thursday morning I became ill. I went anyway, because I hated to have paid for the Seminar and then not attend. It turned out that several there were not feeling well, and God, who knows all things, guided the leaders to start the meeting with prayer instead of the usual Thursday evening meal. The leader of the group, who was to pray for anyone seeking prayer, was a man I had seen at other events. Nearly every time he prayed for a person, the person being prayed for was slain in the Spirit. No way was this going to happen to me. So I waited a while, until another line opened up on the other side of the room. I recognized this leader as a fellow Lutheran, so I got up and walked clear to the other side of the room so that he could pray for me. Sure enough, I immediately fell over by God's Spirit. I knew I didn't fake it, so it had to come from God. I don't really know why God does this, but in this case, it stilled my unbelieving heart.

Eventually, I couldn't wait for the monthly meetings. As a matter of fact, I even started a Full Gospel Chapter in Auburn. The testimonies of the speakers were awesome. Although I was getting more and more enthused for Christ, I continued to struggle in accepting Him enough so others could see a change in me. One day, after we had moved to Auburn, we needed some wallpapering done upstairs. John Mitchell, who was Baptist, was doing the work, and when he found out that Ann was Catholic, he asked her, "Why do you pray to Mary?" She gave the normal Catholic answer that Mary was just a mediator for Christ. John then asked for a Bible and showed her 1 Timothy 2:5: *"For there is one God and one mediator between God and Men, the man Christ Jesus, who gave Himself as a ransom for all men."* This really ministered to Ann, who had been a devoted Catholic all of her life, and as such, had been taught that Mary was the mediator between God and man. She prayed the Rosary every day and had quite a few Catholic statutes all over our house. That verse, however, really challenged her. The next day, I discovered that she had broken and destroyed every statute in the house.

Ann and I had pretty well kept our promise to not ask each other to go to our church, but one March day in about 1974, I asked her if she would attend church with me on Mother's Day. To my shock and amazement, she said yes. It turned out that she wouldn't be attending with me only for Mother's Day, but from then on. She had heard from God that the two of us should attend church together. She even took lessons to become a Lutheran, not because she wanted to, but because she thought she should attend church with me.

At this point, I had become quite enthused about Full Gospel Businessmen, and had even started inviting members of Trinity Lutheran to meetings. This really concerned my Auburn Lutheran pastor. He was quite different from Pastor Hoerger, who had encouraged me to attend the meetings. This pastor started a series in the morning Sunday school classes on 1 Corinthians and Acts, thinking he could convince me that the teachings were taken from the Bible out of context. The class really took scripture out of context, though, and I was getting more and more argumentative in class. When Paul said that speaking in tongues would cease, I believe that he meant when we get to heaven. This class taught that tongues ceased with the book of Acts. One Sunday, December 10, 1976, the pastor came to Ann and me as we left the Sunday school class and asked us to join him in his office. When we got there, we saw that he had also invited the elders to join us.

His first comment was, "Do I understand that you believe in more than one Baptism?"

I replied that he must be referring to water baptism and also Baptism in the Holy Spirit. If so, I said, I certainly did believe in more than one baptism.

He responded that Ephesians 4:5 states that there is *"one Lord, one faith, one Baptism."*

I did not know the Word enough at the time to respond with Acts 1:5: *"For John baptized with water, but in a few days you will be baptized with the Holy Spirit."*

He proceeded to tell me that because of my beliefs, Ann and I could no longer be members of the Lutheran Church. It seemed for a while that this was a horrible day. My dad and my older brother chastised me for some time. But then I came to the realization that what I could not do on my own, the pastor and elders did for me. Now I would be free to go to a church where I could become more engrossed in the word.

We visited a number of churches over the next couple of months. Every Sunday during that period, our family would gather around the dining room table to discuss how we liked the church we had visited that morning. One day I was preparing a tax return for a person I had known attended Victory Life in Fort Wayne. I knew several good families who attended there and who also attended Full Gospel meetings, so I thought that this would probably be the church we finally settled on. Before Sunday came, however, I received a call from the pastor at Calvary Chapel in Hamilton. We had attended his church one of the previous weeks. He suggested that Ann and I go to supper with he and his wife on Saturday night. He said he knew I was a CPA, and wanted my input on some church finance questions he had, so I agreed to meet with them.

On our way to the restaurant, he told me about a family who really needed to find the Lord, and they had attended the church, but he feared that they were not going to follow up. He had heard that they knew me, and it was true that not only did I know this couple, but they also respected me. I immediately said that although I had told a friend that I would be at their church on the following day, I would change plans and go to Calvary Chapel the next day. Immediately there came a war whoop from the back seat exclaiming, "Praise God!" Ann had not explained prior to that moment that she had wanted to make Calvary Chapel our church home. She wanted the decision to be mine, though, which is why she had remained silent on the matter. Learning that made the decision for me. We attended that church for twenty-one years. Ann and I really grew in our relationship with Christ at this small church in Hamilton. The teaching followed God's Word, and the fellowship of believers was great.

Apparently a lot of people were praying for me, because eventually, others began to notice changes in me as well. One of the things we discovered was the truth in God's teachings regarding giving. When I gave three times what I had planned on at a Full Gospel convention, several days later I received a rather substantial payment on an account I had written off as a bad debt some time earlier. When I purchased a parsonage for the Calvary Chapel church, it was hardly any time before my stock investment increased by even more. Several times, God proved to me how true the Scriptures are when they say, *"Give and it will be given to you"* (Luke 6:38). This idea was so contrary to what I had learned in college. I had been taught that if I had $100 and gave away $10, I would have $90. God was teaching me, though, that if I gave to Him with a generous and believing heart, I would truly end up with more, not less. This truth has been emphasized over and over again in our lives, and Ann and I have grown to really believe it.

One time I was preparing to take Ann to another Full Gospel Convention in Detroit. The Sunday before leaving for Detroit, our church asked for a special offering for Jim and Marilyn Olinski. I had budgeted for my trip, and I really did not think that I could afford to give to this also, but I knew it was the right thing to do. Heading to Detroit, I questioned if we would be able to afford all of the activities we would like to do, but we went anyway. Since Ann had a ladies' meeting about the time we arrived at our hotel, I went to our room to plan our evening. I wanted to call Tiger Stadium to see if I could afford a ticket for the game, and when I reached for the phone book, I noticed that it looked like something was inserted in the yellow pages. Upon opening the book, I discovered ten $20 bills.

This troubled me somehow. I tried to figure out what I should do. I reasoned that it wouldn't be sensible to tell the hotel management, since they had no way of knowing how long the money had been there. I thought maybe there was some one who wanted to attend the convention and I was supposed to pay the entry fee for them. But when Ann and I later prayed about what to do, I realized that indeed the money was for my benefit because of my prior week's decision to give in that special offering. God was reminding me once again that it is impossible to out-give Him. I now realize that God had arranged for Ann and me to have the only room in that hotel (at that time, the tallest hotel in the world), to have $200 in the phone book.

God is truly a miraculous God. He has done for my family and me every bit as much as for blind Bartimaeus, for I too was blind, but now I see. Spiritual blindness is much worse than physical blindness. I have pretty good vision despite having one good eye, but now I realize how blind I was.

Another thing that has happened since we both became believing Christians is that Ann and I began recognizing works of God. Prior to knowing Him as I now do, I often attributed His miracles as coincidence. He has since shown us again and again that He is actively at work in our lives. One incident in particular comes to mind as a testimony of God's goodness. In about 1977, Judy was going to Camp Calvary just north of Angola. When Ann and I took her there, we stopped at the camp office building, not knowing which cabin to deliver her to. The bus was just leaving the office building, so they suggested I follow it to the right spot.

Camp Calvary was located in a beautiful place, consisting of curved roads, hills, lakes, and lots of trees. The bus was loaded with other campers, and because of the weight and age of the bus, as well as the curves and rather steep hills, it was struggling to get up the hills. When it reached the top of one of the steep hills, the bus lost its brakes. The bus started coming down the hill toward us, faster and faster, and all the driver could do was honk her horn and pray. Things were happening so fast that we hardly even had time to call on the name of Jesus, which is all you can do in a situation like that. We certainly needed His help, because we were helpless. Our car was behind the bus, just around a curve. It certainly looked like disaster since the bus was probably going fifty miles per hour coming down that hill. If the driver wasn't able to negotiate the curve at the bottom of the hill, the bus would go right into woods. This bus has maybe thirty children on it. If it hit us, not only would we be killed, but all of the children on board would be in danger. And if the bus somehow missed us, it would be nearly impossible for the driver to stop it or miss the hundreds of trees in its path.

I tried to get off the road, but to make the situation even scarier, my engine stalled and I had to restart it. The bus negotiated the curve and was coming straight at us when the driver miraculously turned to her left, barely clipping my left front bumper. The bus then stopped in a soft sandy area right between lots of trees. No one was hurt. However, the driver's response was the most exciting thing of all. She came over to me and apologized for clipping our van; she then said that she had seen this road to the left of me and that a man had directed her onto it. Ann and I both knew that there was no road to the left of my car and certainly no visible person directing traffic. The fact that God would send an angel to protect us in this situation proves just how much He loves us, and is something I will never forget.

The most wonderful miracle of all, however, is His powerful work in my life. I have a wonderful God-believing wife and five delightful children, who are all raising wonderful grandchildren. We are rather certain that all have accepted Christ and desire to witness for Him.

If I had a chance to redo my life, I would change very little. I only wish that I wouldn't have been as stubborn in coming to God, so that I could have begun the victorious years sooner. But I am so very fortunate that God was patient with me. I praise Him daily for my wonderful wife and that I live in a home where my family is so close. All my offspring live in harmony, as do all my grandchildren. Not only is there no arguing in our home or at family get-togethers, but they are indeed joyful occasions. I have live-in help for my wife and myself in the form of family members. I live on a farm that my wife and children love. I had a job that I loved and which provided me with a good income and a great pension.

I have had the opportunity to take incredible vacations and travel extensively. God adopted me as his child. My wife and children love me. What more could I ever have asked for? I pray that upon my death, there is no crying, but only tremendous celebration.

CPSIA information can be obtained
at www.ICGtesting.com
Printed in the USA
FFOW02n1527311016
28920FF

9 781524 638627